Spanish Army of the Napoleonic Wars (2)

1808–12

René Chartrand • Illustrated by Bill Younghusband

Series editor Martin Windrow

First published in Great Britain in 1999 by Osprey Publishing,
Midland House, West Way, Botley, Oxford OX2 0PH, UK
44-02 23rd St, Suite 219, Long Island City, NY 11101, USA
Email: info@ospreypublishing.com

Transferred to digital print on demand 2010

First published 1999
2nd impression 2005

Printed and bound in Great Britain

A CIP catalogue record for this book is available from the British Library

ISBN: 978 1 85532 765 8

Series Editor: Martin Windrow
Design by Alan Hamp/Design for Books

Author's note

This volume is the second of three covering the organization, uniforms and weapons of the Spanish Army in Europe during
the Napoleonic Wars as well as a providing a glimpse of its sea-soldiers; the first, Men-at-Arms 321, covered the period 1793-1808.
This second part deals with the years from late 1808 until 1812, studying the forces which resisted the French invaders with
stubborn determination, almost alone and against all odds. The third part, under preparation as Men-at-Arms 334, will examine
the reorganization of the Spanish army with massive British assistance in the final years of the great struggle against Napoleon's
empire. Based on Spanish as well as newly-discovered British documents, it is hoped that this study will form the most
extensive source yet published in English on the material culture of the Spanish peninsular forces between 1793 and 1815.
See the Select Bibliography at the end of the main text for documentary references to archive material.

The names of Spanish personalities are given in their original Spanish form, thus e.g. King Ferdinand VII is Fernando VII.

Colour hues of Spanish uniforms generally followed practices in other European armies. Thus, blue meant a very dark blue;
similarly, green was very dark, but emerald green was a medium green. Scarlet was indifferently red or scarlet, but crimson
was more reddish than its British counterpart.

Artist's note

Readers may care to note that the original paintings from which the colour plates in this book were prepared are available for
private sale. All reproduction copyright whatsoever is retained by the Publishers. All enquiries should be addressed to:

Bill Younghusband
Moorfield
Kilcolman West
Buttevant
Co.Cork
Eire

The Publishers regret that they can enter into no correspondence upon this matter.

FOR A CATALOGUE OF ALL BOOKS PUBLISHED BY
OSPREY MILITARY AND AVIATION PLEASE CONTACT:

Osprey Direct, c/o Random House Distribution Center,
400 Hahn Road, Westminster, MD 21157
Email: uscustomerservice@ospreypublishing.com

Osprey Direct, The Book Service Ltd, Distribution Centre,
Colchester Road, Frating Green, Colchester, Essex, CO7 7DW
Email: customerservice@ospreypublishing.com

www.ospreypublishing.com

SPANISH ARMY OF THE NAPOLEONIC WARS (2) 1808–12

INTRODUCTION

I N THE SUMMER OF 1808 the Spanish nation was flushed by its incredible victory over General Dupont's French army at Bailen. The standard of revolt had been raised throughout the Iberian peninsula and, thanks to the British fleet, about 9,000 men of General Romana's corps in Denmark had escaped the French and landed in northern Spain. But the French were far from defeated, and their withdrawal into northern Spain was merely a tactical move. An irate Napoleon was assembling his Grand Army to solve the Iberian problem. With a force of over 300,000 men, it was far larger than the effective combined regular forces of Spain, Portugal and Britain deployed in the Peninsula. In October 1808 Napoleon marched into Spain.

On 23 November Marshal Lannes defeated the 45,000-man Spanish army led by General Castaños at Tudela. Another French corps marched into Catalonia and besieged Rosas, which finally fell on 4 December after nearly a month of stubborn resistance. On the same day Napoleon, having defeated all opposition, entered Madrid.

Meanwhile, Sir John Moore's 15,000-strong British army marched from Lisbon into northern Spain to reinforce the hard-pressed Spanish; they reached Sagahun, where British cavalry defeated a French force on 21 December. Although joined by Sir David Baird with another 10,000 British troops, Moore was obliged to retreat towards the coast; Marshal Soult with 80,000 men was closing in fast. After a dreadfully punishing winter retreat Moore's main body arrived at Coruña on 12 January 1809. Soult soon reached the outskirts of this Galician port, and attacked on the 16th. Moore was killed and Baird badly wounded in the battle, but the British managed to escape by sea on the 18th, leaving behind two doomed Spanish regiments who only surrendered on the 20th.

Although this episode had been a sorry lesson in the difficulties of co-operative operations, the British believed that their army had actually saved southern Spain and Portugal from invasion. The Spanish, however, believed that their British allies had retreated hastily to their ships when things got difficult.

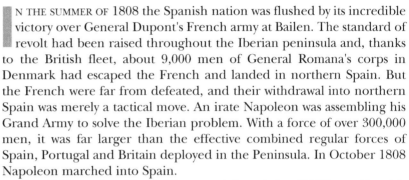

Soldiers, volunteers and even monks in desperate hand-to-hand fighting at the foot of a Pieta in the garden of the Sta.Engracia convent at Zaragoza, 27 January 1809, during the second siege. The painting from which this detail is taken encapsulates the violent intensity which marked the Peninsular War; it is the work of Baron Lejeune, who took part in this action and was wounded close by the statue. (Print after Lejeune)

The Peninsula: the crosshatched areas show the rough extent of the French occupation from 1809 to 1812. The maps of the years 1810 and 1811 show the maximum extent of the French expansion; that of 1812 shows the situation at the end of the year when the Anglo-Portuguese armies finally held their own in the Spanish heartland. The north-eastern corner of Galicia with the port of Coruña escaped effective French control – as, indeed, did much of the country at various periods, since guerrilla activity was ceaseless.

Meanwhile, Spain's central government had collapsed and regional councils or *Juntas* sprang up, with a Central Junta in Sevilla. In Madrid, Napoleon restored his brother Joseph to the Spanish throne, and planned to occupy the Peninsula by brutally stamping out any opposition. Fernando VII, the only lawful king whom the vast majority of Spaniards would recognize, was detained in France. The cause of independence might have seemed hopeless to observers; but this was Spain, and desperate fighting continued into 1809.

One heroic example was the defence of the city of Zaragoza. First besieged unsuccessfully between June and August 1808, the city suffered a second siege by French forces led by (successively) Marshals Moncey, Mortier, Junot and Lannes from 20 December 1808. The Spanish defenders, galvanized by General José Palafox, put up a fanatical resistance against all odds. The whole populace joined the regular soldiers and militiamen in defending their city, even women and monks taking up arms to join a fight of a ferocity unparalleled in the annals of the Peninsular War. Eventually, epidemic fevers broke out and many thousands died of sickness; but the survivors, huddled in cellars during bombardments, came out fighting to the death. Finally Palafox, too, fell ill, still issuing orders from his sickbed until overcome by delirium. On 21 February 1809 the half-destroyed city of Zaragoza at last surrendered. The casualties were horrendous, and the church square was covered with coffins and dead bodies. An estimated 48,000 Spanish men, women and children had died of pestilence, and another 6,000 in combat. The French had lost about 10,000 soldiers. The city's pre-war population of 55,000 had been reduced to about 15,000 souls. However, as Sir Charles Oman later correctly observed, the 'example of Zaragoza was invaluable to the nation and to Europe. The knowledge of it did much to sicken the French soldiery of the whole war, and to make every officer and man who entered Spain march, not with the light heart that he felt in Germany or Italy, but with gloom and disgust and want of confidence.'

A few months later the French besieged Gerona in Catalonia, again meeting heroic resistance from the Spanish soldiers and citizens. The siege lasted from 24 May to 11 December 1809, leaving 14,000 Spanish dead – half of them civilians – and 13,000 French soldiers. New Spanish levies had been raised, often commanded by inexperienced officers, without proper logistics. They had a few successes before the Central Junta ordered the main Spanish army of 53,000 men led by General Areizaga to free Madrid; this force was crushed by Marshal Soult at

Ocaña, Castille, on 17 November. This disaster wiped out a large part of Spain's organized forces and opened the way to Andalucia, which the French immediately invaded. With about 30,000 men left to fight off over 60,000 French troops, resistance in Andalucia collapsed. The Central Junta resigned power to an elected Cortes (or legislative assembly), which took refuge in Cadiz as the advancing French invested the city on 5 February 1810. Reinforced by British and Portuguese troops, Cadiz was to remain under siege from the landward side for two-and-a-half years. Thanks to Britain's Royal Navy, however, its port remained open.

The French now controlled nearly all of Spain except for parts of Galicia, Valencia and Catalonia. By October 1810 they had penetrated as far as the fortified lines of Torres Vedras near Lisbon, and were still in central Portugal in March 1811 before they were forced to withdraw. It took the rest of the year for Wellington's and Beresford's Anglo-Portuguese force, assisted by a Spanish corps, to establish solid positions in the Spanish provinces of Extremadura and Leon.

In this propaganda painting, the Emperor Napoleon receives the surrender of Madrid in early December 1808 from a group of supplicant Spanish emissaries. In fact, nothing could have been further from the truth: the Spanish people were mobilising for one of the most determined resistances against an invader in history. (Print after Vernet)

RESISTANCE AND BRITISH AID

The Spanish army, in spite of repeated defeats from late 1808 onwards, was never completely destroyed. Three further factors worked with success against the French: the guerrillas, the 'armed peasantry' or volunteers, and British material assistance.

Of these, the phenomenon of the guerrillas was certainly the most novel. Guerrilla groups had risen spontaneously since late 1808 to operate behind the French lines, using their knowledge of Spain's mountainous topography to advantage. Motivated largely by a hatred of the marauding French soldiers' wanton robbery, pillage, murder and rape among the civilian population, many guerrilla bands wreaked revenge of medieval savagery upon any unfortunate French soldiers they captured. By 1810 some guerrilla groups had become small armies of several thousand men.

The armed peasantry and volunteers were not guerrillas, although they are sometimes confused with them. They appeared in the countryside and in towns to assist the regular and provincial troops. Good examples of such organizations were the city volunteer units in Cadiz, and the rural armed peasantry of the Galician 'Alarm' groups.

British aid was certainly a major factor in fuelling the Spanish resistance. Between May 1808 and May 1809 alone, supplies to Spain from England included 155 artillery pieces, 200,277 muskets, 39,000 sets of accoutrements, 61,391 swords, 79,000 pikes, 40,000 tents, 50,000 canteens, 54,000 knapsacks, 92,100 uniforms, shoes, and hats, nearly half a million yards of linen, calico and wool, along with £1,412,354 in cash and bills of exchange (to put this figure in perspective, in 1808 Britain's total expenditure on her large and strategically vital Royal Navy was £17,496,047). These supplies were usually shipped to Gijon, Coruña and Cadiz. For example, on 27 August 1808 some 24,000 suits of clothing, 20,000 knapsacks with pouches and belts, 10,000 shakos and pairs of shoes were bound for Gijon. At the same time 6,000 suits of clothing, round hats and cockades, gaiters, pouches and belts, 4,000 knapsacks and 10,000 pairs of shoes were intended for Coruña; while a large shipment of 'blue, white [and] red' fabrics 'for clothing 50,000 men' with serge, linen and calico were shipping for Cadiz (PRO, WO 1/841, WO 6/164). In the autumn of 1808 some 12,000 green uniforms faced with red, 8,000 blue uniforms faced with red, and 4,000 red coatees, white waistcoats and grey pantaloons were sent to Asturias (PRO, FO 72/69).

This aid went on unabated for years, with tens of thousands of items of armament, ammunition, uniforms and equipment being shipped every month to meet the huge demands of Spanish juntas and patriots. These demands were, in large part, met. In August 1809 we find (PRO, AO 16/61) 'to...the Marquis de la Romana... for the use of Spanish troops under his command 10,000

General José Palafox, the indomitable leader of the defence of Zaragoza. He and his family were to suffer from Napoleon's cruelty until the end of the war. The incredibly stubborn resistance of the city in 1809 enraged Napoleon; although the surrendering garrison had been granted the honours of war, he had Marshal Lannes arrest Palafox as a political prisoner and imprisoned him in the castle of Vincennes, spreading a rumour that he had died in prison. His release in 1814 provoked much joy throughout Spain. (Print after portrait)

muskets with bayonets and steel rammers, extra repaired of sorts, 10,000 musket bayonet scabbards, 10,000 black infantry accoutrements' with ammunition. In December 1810 four 12pdr. cannons, four 8pdr. cannons, four 4pdr. cannons, 8,000 muskets with accoutrements, 4,000 sabres, 20,000 pairs of shoes, 10,000 suits of clothing comprising jacket, pantaloons, waistcoat, gaiters and shirts, and 5,000 greatcoats were all sent to Asturias (PRO, WO 1/261). These were in addition to tens of thousands of muskets and uniforms sent earlier during 1810. By 1811 the policy was to supply arms, clothing, and ammunition for 42,000 men of the Spanish army which, at this time, was reckoned to total about 90,000 men. Wellington also had an annual sum of £1 million to supply the needs of Spanish troops operating in conjunction with or under the command of the British forces.

However, even these very large shipments were far from enough; Spanish armies were often clad in brown peasants' clothes for lack of uniforms.

British attitudes

Senior British officers and officials in Spain were often unjust in their sweeping condemnations of the quality of Spanish troops and the character of the Spanish people. This attitude spread to the lower ranks, as countless journals of British officers and private soldiers testify. One explanation, perhaps, was that these men came from a Britain which was experiencing the world's first industrial revolution, a country they

LEFT **A heavy cavalry regiment, possibly the Infante Regiment in General Romana's Corps, c.1808-1809, wearing blue coats with light buff or white collar, lapels and turnbacks, brass buttons, white breeches, and blue housings edged red. (Print after J.Booth)**

RIGHT **A light cavalry regiment wearing green uniforms with red collars, shoulder straps and plumes, white cords and lace – possibly the Cazadores de Olivenza Regiment in Romana's Corps, c.1808-1809. Their uniform was emerald green hussar-style jackets with scarlet collar and cuffs (see MAA 321) from 1808 until about 1811. In Mallorca in July 1812 Lieutenant Woolcombe noted that they wore 'yellow jackets, red cuff and cape (collar), helmet like the British light dragoons, red feather' – which was obviously a Tarleton helmet. (Print after J.Booth)**

believed to be at the forefront of scientific, economic, and social progress. While our concept of democracy was unknown, a recognition of mutual dependency between the social classes had given Britain an army in which all ranks were united by an instinctive patriotism – particularly when they found themselves on alien shores. Any comparison based on personal experience was bound to reflect unfavourably upon Spain, which they perceived as a poor, semi-feudal, agrarian and narrow-minded society; and generalizing from personal experience was and is the universal vice of the ignorant. The Spanish responded by reminding their English allies as to exactly who was doing the huge majority of the fighting in Spain while they were busy in Portugal.

Worse – and regarded as intolerable by the Spanish – British commanders were suspected of plotting to put Spanish troops under British officers, as had been done in Portugal; and it was true. In June 1810 Lord Wellesley, Wellington's elder brother and the British ambassador to the Cortes, had written a 'Memorandum on a Spanish Army' which outlined the organization of a corps in British pay totalling 30,000 men 'which might be clothed in red'. The plan was based on the premise that 'Spaniards are capable of being made into good soldiers as any in the world; that they are perhaps the cheapest soldiers which Great Britain can employ; and that they would serve with confidence and ardour under the command of British officers', of which there were to be 144 including all senior officers (*Supplementary Dispatches*, VII). When, in March 1811, Wellesley suggested that Spanish provinces on the Portuguese border be put under the authority of Wellington, Spanish feelings were aroused and rumours spread about the Spanish army being placed under British officers. The resentment was such that, in August, Wellesley made a statement to the Cortes denying everything as vile rumours. The Spanish gracefully accepted his statement, and kept an eye on their ally. And not without reason; in September 1812 another proposal to raise brigades of Spanish soldiers 'to be commanded and in part officered by British officers' came from no less than the Duke of York, commander-in-chief of the British forces, who asked the Secretary of War Lord Bathurst to seek the views of the Duke of Wellington (PRO, WO 6/36). The Spanish would have been outraged, as Bathurst and Wellington well knew, and nothing came of it.

However, a number of British officers and soldiers were also ardent supporters of the Spanish effort and admirers of Spain and her people. Men such as John Downie (who raised, partly at his own cost, the Extremadura Legion), Charles Doyle and William Parker Carroll, to cite a few of the better known officers who operated with the Spanish troops in the interior, were unequivocal hispanophiles. Far away from the British lines, they brought great sympathy, hope and assistance to the Spanish, who greeted them with open arms.

Possibly the strongest and least prejudiced allies of the Spanish were the Ministers of the British government. They sensed the continuing embarrassment caused by the valiant Spanish resistance to Napoleon's 'invincible' armies. Their support would also have been motivated by the generally favourable popular opinion towards Spain's struggle held among the British public. Perhaps they also perceived that something was changing in the 'Art of War' with the emergence of truly effective guerrilla warfare. Thus, in spite of unfavourable comments by British officers in the field frustrated by undeniable shortcomings, the Spanish were to be helped at all costs.

'At all costs' was far from easy to achieve. Although Britain was a 'rich' country, its finances were stretched to the limit by a national debt of over £606 million, an enormous sum for the time. In 1811, of £91 million expenditures, interest payments alone took nearly £36 million – over half of the £64 million of revenue. Thus, nearly £30 million had to be borrowed to meet the demands of what was in some senses a world war. It was in this context that somehow, through the constant efforts of Lord Castlereagh, Lord Liverpool, Lord Bathurst, George Canning and many others, millions of pounds were found annually to finance and supply the Spanish. It was a good investment because, in spite of an occupying French army of some 300,000 men, the Spanish simply could not be put down. However, until 1812 the aid from Britain, although considerable, was not sufficient to keep the Spanish army tolerably well supplied.

The state of the Spanish armies

Both French and British officers who observed the Spanish troops often noted the same faults and the same qualities. Generally, if for different motives, the French and British noted that the Spanish tended to make

At left, a trooper of the Granaderos a Caballo Fernando VII, 1808-1812. Raised as 'Horse Grenadiers of Fernando VII' from 8 September 1808 by Count Fernan-Nunez, with 540 men in three squadrons, they were converted into 'Fernando VII Hussars' from 1 May 1811. The unit had a bearskin colpack with a red plume at the side and a silver oval plate with an 'F VII' cipher (Pacheco shows a shako in 1810). The green coatee has yellow collar and cuffs, red turnbacks, three rows of pewter buttons, white lace between the buttons and edging the collar and cuffs, and a white '7' on the collar; the brown overalls have pewter buttons on the red stripe and leather strapping. The green housing is edged with white lace. (continued opposite)

ponderous and largely predictable tactical moves. The British, who most appreciated steadfastness under fire and near-clockwork movements, were often appalled by what they perceived as undisciplined and badly-drilled formations moving about the field, and often decamping rather hastily in the face of enemy pressure. The French, who admired the massive yet speedy movements of their formations followed by furious charges at bayonet- and sword-point, often found that the Spanish offered an incredibly fierce resistance that might collapse suddenly. The resulting Spanish losses, both in battle and during pursuit after such collapses, tended to be proportionately higher.

It is clear that the 'laissez-faire' years of neglect under Carlos IV's prime minister Manuel Godoy were now bearing bitter fruit. Spain, invaded by large numbers of French troops, found that its army was out-numbered and outskilled. Both British and French observers agreed on the basic quality of the Spanish soldier, a tough, cheerful and ever-enduring individual often living in conditions far worse than his British or French counterparts. They also noticed the general ineptitude of the Spanish officers, whom they regarded as vain and ignorant. Certainly, the battlefield performance reflected this in its most important aspect: firepower. Spanish battalion fire was found to be unsteady and slow (much to the relief of the French and the alarm of the British). In 1809, for instance, Lieutenant-Colonel Symes observed that Spanish troops would give fire twice a minute as opposed to the usual three volleys per minute. And when they did fire, the Spanish volleys often had more misfires than their opponents.

Such observations go a long way to explaining the usual lack of success by Spanish battalions in open field fighting. Not only did the French often appear in superior numbers, but their fire was more effective by at least one third. French and British chroniclers, and countless historians since, laid the blame squarely on the Spanish officer corps. As Captain Lovell Badcock of the 14th Light Dragoons put it, the Spanish were 'not bad looking troops, but I fear, ill commanded'.

Officer, Caballeria de Fernando 7, 1810. This was probably a member of the Granaderos a Caballo Fernando VII detached in Cadiz. Except for a shako instead of a bearskin cap the uniform is similar, consisting of a green coatee with yellow collar and cuffs, white lace, silver epaulettes and buttons, and a black shako with silver cords. Watercolour by Antonio Pareira Pacheco. (Biblioteca Publica Municipal, Santa Cruz de Tenerife, Canary Islands)

What seems less widely known is that the Spanish themselves largely recognized that the lack of officer training was a serious problem. They realized that specialized military education had to be provided at once, even during the period of invasion and occupation; and they did something about it. A number of military academies for training aspiring young officers appeared from nowhere from 1808. It is obvious that in spite of enormous difficulties, these were serious and determined institutions of learning. The quality of courses provided in these academies must have varied in such desperate times; some were obliged to move around the country only a step ahead of the rambling French armies. In 1811 the Cortes took the important decision to abolish the requirement that officers should come from the nobility, and these schools became open to all talents. That same year a training centre for enlisted men was set up by Colonel Doyle in Cadiz, and the Cortes decreed the principle of universal service. Hampered, however, by a nearly empty treasury, a haphazard supply system, and the great difficulties of co-ordination due to the French occupation and local politics, all this could only have a limited effect.

The Spanish forces were divided into regional armies. In October 1808 the front-line armies were the Army of Galicia, the Army of Aragon, the Army of Extremadura, the Army of the Centre, and the Army of Catalonia. The reserve armies were the Army of Granada, the Galician Reserves, the Asturian Reserves, the Army of Reserve of Madrid, the Extremadurian Reserves, and the Balearic Islands, Murcian, Valencian and Andalucian Reserves. There were many changes thereafter, but the regional identification remained until December 1811. Although the Spanish forces were by then organized into Armies of the Centre, the Left and the Right, these grouped the armies of Catalonia (much of it destroyed at Tarragona in July), Valencia, Murcia, Extremadura and Galicia plus various formations such as the Majorca Division.

UNIFORMS AND EQUIPMENT

The Spanish armies of 1808 and 1809 were not always ill-armed and in rags. In October 1808 Charles Vaughan, a British diplomat, described part of the Spanish Army of Aragon as full of well-dressed and fine-looking men. The exception was the O'Neille Division with only one infantry regiment in uniform, with the rest dressed in local cloaks over a shirt and light trousers and sandals for footwear, but uniforms were expected to arrive any day. He then reported that part of General Castaños' Army of Andalucia was well-dressed, with a very soldierly bearing.

In April 1809 Britain supplied clothing for 50,000 Spanish troops. Some 25,000 sets were shipped to Cadiz, of which 15,000 were blue coatees and 10,000 white coatees, all with scarlet collars, cuffs and lapels and brass buttons; they were accompanied with white waistcoats and breeches and black gaiters. A month later, all units in the recently organized Ballesteros Division, part of the Asturias Army then at Contrueces, Gijon, were issued with 20,000 uniforms and 25,000 pairs of shoes from England. The division's Castrapol Regiment had white uniforms with scarlet facings, and it may be that the whole supply was in these colours. But many troops were now dressing in brown, blue, green, and red instead of white. By August 1809 clothing had become so varied among the Spanish troops that Wellington felt 'an exertion ought to be made immediately to clothe them in the national uniform', adding that if 'the whole army wore the national uniform, it would be possible to disgrace those who misbehave, either by depriving them of it or by affixing some mark to it'.

The national uniform was not to be for a while. In late November 1809 many grey and some blue jackets were sent, along with shakos and cockades; other clothing of unspecified colours was also shipped. In November 1810 some 12,000 suits of clothing 'to be sky blue', with 20,000 greatcoats and haversacks, 40,000 pairs of shoes, half-stockings and shirts, and 1,000 pairs of boots were ordered sent to 'the Army in Catalonia' along with 10,000 stands of arms (PRO, WO 6/206).

By 1811 blue was obviously becoming the new colour for the Spanish infantry. Sky or light blue was apparently predominant at first, but 'blue' (meaning dark blue) became the preferred colour by the end of that year. In May the army in Catalonia was shipped '8,000 suits of light blue clothing' with 12,000 pairs of half-gaiters (PRO, WO 1/848). In October Wellington wrote of 'a division of infantry, now raising in Castille, under Don Carlos de España, to which I have supplied arms and accoutrements', and that it 'may be supplied with blue clothing... as soon as possible' (Dispatches, VIII).

The style of the British clothing sent to Spain appears usually to have been a simple single-breasted coatee or jacket, with collar and cuffs in a contrasting facing or the jacket colour. Waistcoats generally seem to have been of white kersey, pantaloons usually of the jacket colour. Shakos were favoured by the Spanish from 1809; they were usually wider at the top than the base and fairly plain. The 'caps & cockades' from Britain often appear to have been in that style, sent plain except for the cockade. Naturally, many 'improvements' could be added by regimental tailors, and this appears to have become common after 1812.

Generals and Staff
The regulation uniforms of general officers remained officially the same as described in MAA 321, but there were some changes in fashion. The generals still wore blue but, especially in more formal dress or on campaign, might have worn an all-blue coat without lapels, and with gold embroidery edging the collar, front, cuffs and pocket flaps.

On 9 June 1810 a *Cuerpo de Estado Mayor* or General Staff Corps of 62 officers was created to improve staff work; it was increased to 134 officers in January 1811. (See Plate F for uniforms.)

Line infantry grenadiers, c.1808-1809. They wear the tall bearskin caps with long, embroidered bags distinctive of Spanish grenadiers. (Print after J. Booth)

In 1810 some of the rank badges for garrison staff officers were simplified. The *Teniente del Rey* (King's Lieutenant, in effect a lieutenant-governor) was to be distinguished by two gold laces each 3.5cm wide. The *Sargento Mayor de Plaza* (Town Mayor) had one 2.9cm gold lace.

In July 1810 the introduction of the new ranks of battalion commander for foot troops, and squadron commander for cavalry and dragoons, brought a new rank badge: one gold lace and one silver, no matter what the unit's lace colour. This rank was in between that of major (one gold or silver lace) and lieutenant-colonel (two gold or silver laces).

Cavalry

The organization of cavalry regiments changed on 1 October 1808. Each regiment was now to have four squadrons, each of three companies. Each company had one captain, one lieutenant, one ensign, three sergeants, four corporals, one trumpeter, 42 mounted troopers, and 11 dismounted troopers. Each regiment had a staff of eight field officers, four standard bearers, a marshal major, a chaplain, a surgeon, a trumpet major, a kettledrummer and a *picador*. On 30 January 1809 the establishment of troopers per company was raised to 81. On 23 April 1809 the composition was changed to eight corporals, 48 mounted troopers and 11 dismounted. The staff had nine field officers, four standard bearers, a marshal major, a chaplain, a surgeon, a trumpet major, a kettledrummer, a master saddler, a master armourer and a picador. On 15 July 1809 each regiment was reduced by one squadron; but by then all this was largely theoretical.

From 1808 many new squadrons of heavy and light cavalry were raised or reorganized from older formations. The deficiencies in men and horses often meant a much lower actual strength; only one squadron was actually mounted, the two others serving on foot as infantry. Yet new units also appeared, including many of line cavalry (such as the Voluntarios de Sevilla, Voluntarios de Ciudad Rodrigo, Carabineros Reales de Extremadura, Perseguidos de Andalucia, 2nd Alcantara, Cruzada de Alberquerque, 2nd Santiago, Cuenca, and the 2nd Algarve); of dragoons (Caceres, Castilla, Madrid, Granada, 2nd Luisitania, and Soria); of *cazadores* (Granada, Valencia, Sevilla, Fuen-Santa, Sagrario de Toledo, Mantañas de Cordoba, 1st and 2nd Squadrons of Francos de Castilla, Navarra, Mancha, Ubrique, Jaen, Galicia, and Madrid); of hussars (1st and 2nd Extremadura, Granada, Daroca later Aragon, San Narciso later Cataluña, Rioja, Iberia, Navarra, Francos de Castilla, Burgos, and Numantinos); of mounted grenadiers (Fernando VII, and Galicia), of cuirassiers (Coraceros Españoles), and of lancers (Utrera, 1st Castilla, and Legion Estremeña).

Line infantry fusiliers, c.1808-1809. The figure at left wears the standard uniform; his comrade relaxes in his forage cap and sandals while smoking a long white cigarette. (Print after J.Booth)

On 6 April 1811 a regulation from the Cortes in Cadiz tried to organize the multitude of units, and decreed that the regular cavalry would consist of 12 regiments of heavy cavalry (Rey, Reina, Principe, Infante, Borbon, Faresio, Alcantara, España, Algarve, Calatrava, Santiago, and Montesa); ten of dragoons (Rey, Reina, Almansa, Pavia, Villaviciosa, Sagunto, Numancia, Luisitania, Granada, and Madrid); four of cazadores (Olivenza, Voluntarios de España, Sevilla, and Valencia); and four of hussars (Extremadura, Españoles, Granada, and Fernando VII).

There were also regular provincial squadrons: one of heavy cavalry (Cuenca), one of cazadores (Ubrique), one of dragoons (Soria) and five of hussars (Cataluña, Aragon, Galicia, Cantabria, and Castilla). In addition to these units there were also the Coraceros Españoles, and some of the larger guerrilla groups also maintained cavalry units, such as the Iberia Hussars raised by El Medico. It is impossible to list all units; but those mentioned below and in the illustrations and plates will give an idea of the diversity of the Spanish cavalry corps serving between 1808 and 1812.

Dragones del General Company Formed by General Joaquin Blake after General Cuesta's defeat at Medina de Rioseco on 14 July 1808, with survivors of the Colorados de Buenos Aires Battalion (see below), who were best suited for mounted service. They dressed in typical South American 'gaucho' style with the poncho-like *chirispas,* and when on patrol would try to rope French soldiers with their *lazos.* The dragoons fought at Astorga, Tamanos and Ciudad Rodrigo, after which the troop was dissolved, the remaining men being sent back to Montevideo in 1812.

Cazadores de Olivenza With four squadrons in Valencia in 1808 totalling 37 officers and 558 men, they fought the French in many engagements including Bailen and Tudela, and were nearly wiped out at Maria. They were reconstituted in three squadrons and saw action again from November 1809 in Barcelona and Valencia province. Part of the regiment helped form the Granada Hussars in June 1808, the Coraceros Españoles in July 1810, and the Cazadores de Valencia in March 1811. Transferred to Mallorca in April 1811, two squadrons landed at Alicante in 1812, and one remained at Mallorca, but all three were in the Peninsula in 1813 campaigning in General Whittingham's Mallorca Division. They became the Costa de Granada Line Cavalry Regiment on 1 December 1814. For uniform see accompanying illustration.

Extremadura Hussars The Maria Luisa Hussars were amalgamated to form the 1st and 2nd Extremadura Hussars (raised in 1808) and later united into Extremadura Hussars. Uniform was an all sky blue dolman, a scarlet pelisse and pantaloons, with pewter buttons, white cords, and emerald green housings edged white.

At left, a light infantry fusilier, c.1808, wearing the crested cap with a yellow band and green plume, and the old green jacket faced red with yellow cords. At right, a gunner in blue faced with red. (Print after J.Booth)

RIGHT **This print of the surrender of Tarragona show the Spanish troops wearing tall busbies with hanging bags, and a lapelled coatee. As it was the work of Pierre Martinet, who published large numbers of good uniform prints between c.1807 and the 1830s, and as these details are shown in several of his other prints of Spanish battles, it is likely that they were reported to him by French soldiers who had served in Spain.**

Charles W.Doyle was a British liaison officer sent into Spain in 1808. With considerable energy and enthusiasm, he managed to obtain some supplies for the Spanish forces in northern Spain, and raised the Tiradores de Doyle, with whom he fought gallantly in many engagements. Recalled in 1811, he was retained in Cadiz to organize and command a large training centre for the Spanish army.

San Narcisso/Cataluña Hussars Raised from 15 December 1809 as San Narcisso Hussars during the siege of Gerona, their name was later changed to Cataluña Hussars, and they were incorporated into the Numancia Dragoons on 1 October 1814.

Uniform was an all sky blue dolman, a green pelisse edged with brown fur, yellow cords, brass buttons, a scarlet and yellow hussar sash, sky blue breeches, and a tall, visored, conical black cap with a white wing edged scarlet and a red plume.

Lanceros de Extremadura See Legion Extremadura below.

Infantry

In 1808 the line infantry was organized into regiments of three battalions, each of four companies of fusiliers except for the 1st Battalion, which had two companies of grenadiers. The war establishment of each regiment was theoretically over 2,300 officers and men, but the actual strength was much lower. Light infantry battalions had six companies totalling a theoretical war establishment of over 1,300 officers and men, but this too exceeded the real figures.

The war of independence against the French saw a multitude of new units created. Between May and December 1808 some 210 regiments, 48

Officer of the Regimiento de Fernando VII, 1810. The infantry Regimiento de Leales de Fernando VII was raised from 3 September 1808 and fought at Talavera on 27 July 1809; in 1810 its 1st Battalion was in Cadiz while the 2nd and 3rd campaigned in Extremadura. This man wears a blue coatee with scarlet collar and cuffs, white piping, silver epaulettes and buttons, white breeches, and a black shako with silver lace and plate. Watercolour by Antonio Pareira Pacheco. (Biblioteca Publica Municipal, Santa Cruz de Tenerife, Canary Islands)

of which were light infantry, were listed. In 1809 another 18 line and 16 light infantry regiments were formed. The variety in organization of these units, raised spontaneously all over the country, was naturally considerable, and in 1810 some standardization was attempted.

On 1 July 1810 it was decreed that the regular infantry would consist of eight battalions of grenadiers, formed from the remnants of the provincial militia grenadier battalions; 121 regiments of line infantry, which incorporated the provincial militia regiments; 32 battalions of light infantry; and Swiss regiments as necessary.

The grenadier battalions were to have 681 men in four companies of grenadiers and one of light infantry; each company was to have a captain, two lieutenants, one sub-lieutenant, four sergeants, three drummers, 12 corporals and 111 privates. The battalion staff consisted of a lieutenant-colonel, one major, two lieutenant-adjutants, one ensign, one chaplain, one surgeon, one armourer and a drum major.

Line infantry regiments were to have 2,554 men in three battalions, each battalion having a company of grenadiers, a company of cazadores (chasseurs or light company), and four companies of fusiliers. Each grenadier company was to have a captain, two lieutenants, one sub-lieutenant, four sergeants, two drummers, two fifers, ten corporals and 91 privates. Each cazador company was to have a captain, two lieutenants, one sub-lieutenant, four sergeants, two drummers, ten corporals and 85 privates. Each fusilier company to have a captain, two lieutenants, two sub-lieutenants, five sergeants, three drummers, 16 corporals and 136 privates. The battalion staff consisted of a colonel and a major in the 1st Battalion, a lieutenant-colonel in the 2nd, and a commandant in the 3rd, each battalion having a lieutenant-adjutant, one ensign, one chaplain, one surgeon, one armourer and a drum major.

Light infantry battalions were to have six companies of fusiliers totalling 1,201 men. Each company was to have a first captain, a second captain, two lieutenants, two sub-lieutenants, six sergeants, four drummers, 20 corporals and 170 privates. The battalion staff consisted of a commandant, a major, a captain-adjutant, a lieutenant-adjutant, one ensign, one chaplain, one surgeon, one armourer and a drum major.

On 19 October 1811 two *cornetas* or buglers replaced two drummers in each cazador company in infantry regiments and in all companies of the light infantry battalions. At this time the French-style bugle horns were replaced by British bugles; at first the Spanish found these much harder to use, but soon preferred them because they could be heard at a much greater distance.

The official establishments of the regiments and battalions were, like the previous organization, much too optimistic. The decree called for some 361,000 men in the infantry alone, quite apart from cavalry, artillery and other corps, not to mention guerrillas. It led to another reorganization in March 1812 which better reflected the reality. Many units were short-lived and left little surviving data; they cannot all be listed in this work, but those described below and in the illustrations and plates give a fair idea of the diversity of their service and appearance.

Princesa Fought at Gebora and Saguntum in 1811 and at Salamanca in 1812. The uniform was white with violet facings at the beginning of the war. From 1809 to 1811 it consisted of a blue coatee with white lapels, violet collar and cuffs, linen pantaloons, and a brown greatcoat lined with linen.

Diana.

Officer of the Real Guardias Españolas, 1810. Some 900 men of the Spanish Guards Regiment were at the second siege of Zaragoza in 1808-1809. The 2nd and 4th battalions managed to reach Cadiz in early 1810 and thereafter took part in the city's defence; they were also at Albuera in 1811. The uniform consisted of a blue coatee and trousers, with blue collar, scarlet cuffs and turnbacks, white lace and waistcoat, silver epaulettes, and a black shako with silver lace and plate and red plume. Watercolour by Antonio Pareira Pacheco. (Biblioteca Publica Municipal, Santa Cruz de Tenerife, Canary Islands)

Hibernia This 'Irish' regiment was in Galicia in 1808, and scattered into the mountains with other Spanish units while Sir John Moore's army evacuated Coruña in January 1809. General Romana regrouped and reorganized the Galician army, and gave the colonelcy of Hibernia to William Parker Carroll, his Irish-born British liaison officer. With great energy and success, Parker Carroll reconstructed first one and eventually two battalions.

Hibernia took part in Romana's capture of Villafranca and Vigo, the failed siege of Lugo, the repulse of Marshal Ney's forces at San Payo bridge and, on 8 October 1809, the utter defeat of the French VI Corps at Tamames. Reinforced French troops defeated the Galician army on 28 November at Alba de Tormes, Hibernia being one of the few regiments to firmly maintain its squares against the French cavalry. Hibernia retreated into Extremadura with the Galician army, and was part of the Spanish contingent sent by Romana in October 1810 to assist Wellington in the Torres Vedras position during Marshal Masséna's invasion of Portugal.

When Marshal Soult invaded Extremadura in February 1811 Hibernia was one of the units sent to the rescue, only to be crushed and almost destroyed at Gebora (19 February). Survivors escaped to Portugal, and Parker Carroll resurrected it with Castillian recruits. From February 1812 to the end of the war it remained in Ciudad Rodrigo. The regiment, now completely Spanish, was disbanded in 1818.

The regiment's sky blue uniform had worn out by November 1808, the men being 'dressed almost entirely in the costume of their native mountains' (PRO, WO 1/233). This would have been a brown short jacket, waistcoat, breeches, leggings and a cloak – the last being indispensable. In July 1809 Parker Carroll asked Lord Liverpool for 'scarlet jacket, green facings, yellow buttons' and 'regimental caps (shakos) with red plumes', with pantaloons and equipment. The request is interesting in that it shows the change in uniform colours and the adoption of shakos by Spanish troops. There is no evidence that these uniforms were sent, however, although canteen straps, linen shirts and shoes were shipped from Britain specifically to the Hibernia Regiment in August 1810 (PRO, WO 1/241 and /845).

Cangas de Onis Single-battalion regiment of 840 men raised in Asturias from 27 May 1808; it was incorporated into the 1st Asturias Regiment on 9 May 1812. The uniform in c.1808-1809 consisted of a white jacket with blue collar, cuffs and piping, pewter buttons, white breeches, and a white forage cap with a blue band.

Llanes Single-battalion regiment of 840 men raised in Asturias from 27 May 1808 and incorporated into the 2nd Asturias Regiment on 14 April 1811. The uniform was a brown coatee with sky blue collar, cuffs and piping, pewter buttons, white breeches, a bicorn with a sky blue plume, and black accoutrements.

Voluntarios de la Victoria Two-battalion light infantry regiment raised in El Ferol, Galicia, from 11 June 1808, its early recruits being officers and men from the Navy. It saw much action in the Basque provinces in the autumn, campaigned in Castille in 1809, Portugal in 1810, Extremadura in 1811, Castilla in 1812, was at the battle of Vittoria in 1813, in southern France in 1814 and was sent to America in 1815. For the uniform see the accompanying illustration.

Buenos Aires This unit had its origins in the British attacks on the Rio de la Plata in Argentina and Uruguay in January 1807. Initially successful, the British force captured Montevideo taking some 800 Spanish colonial regulars prisoner. They were sent to prison hulks in England, but following the Spanish uprising against the French in May 1808 they were shipped to Coruña and formed into a Buenos Aires Battalion during June. According to Captain (later General) Rondeau, they were issued British arms and uniforms consisting of 'red coatees, white waistcoats and breeches', which earned them the nickname *Colorados* – 'the reds'. Attached to General Cuesta's army which was defeated at Medina de Rioseco on 14 July, the battalion was decimated. The unit was reorganized, however, and reportedly lacked uniforms when in Galicia in January 1812 (PRO, AO 16/69).

Tiradores de Doyle/Cazadores de Barbastros A light infantry battalion of 300 men raised from 10 August 1808 in Galicia by Colonel Charles W.Doyle, a British officer sent to help the insurgents. It apparently had 1,200 men in ten companies in May 1810. Doyle led his unit in many actions, and was wounded several times, earning much renown for himself and his men. Doyle was promoted general and recalled to other duties in 1811; his unit, renamed Cazadores de Barbastros (after the unit raised in 1794) continued under Antonio Guerrerro (however, the old name of 'Doyle's' was still used). The corps fought at Albuera and Saguntum in 1811, and had grown to about 1,400 men by 1812. The early uniforms seem to have been red with white waistcoats and breeches, probably with round hats. In May 1810 the men had each received 'a hat, cloth jacket, 2 shirts, a pair of trousers, a pair of country shoes' while at Gibraltar (PRO, WO 1/1120). Later on, '1,400 suits for Doyle's Regiment' were ordered by Wellington in August 1812.

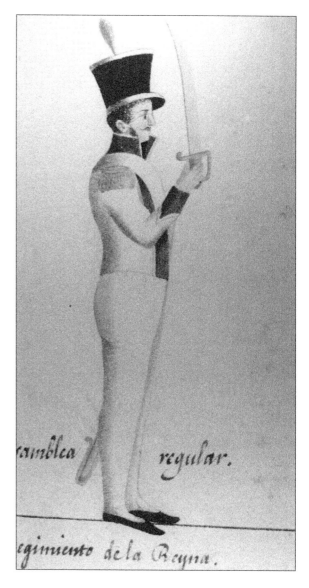

Officer of the Reina/Galicia Regiment, 1810. The Reina Regiment, which had been called Galicia until 1792, was posted at Malaga in 1808 and was part of General Castaños' army at the battle of Bailen. It later moved to Cadiz and formed part of the city's garrison. On 3 March 1810 it reverted to its old name of Galicia. According to this Pacheco watercolour, its white uniform had sky blue cuffs, lapels, and collar (rather than violet), white piping, and a shako with a wide top. (Biblioteca Publica Municipal, Santa Cruz de Tenerife, Canary Islands)

Officer of the Defensores de la Patria, 1810 (the unit's full name was Regimiento de linea Defensores Veterano de la Patria). It arrived in Cadiz on 4 February 1810, and remained there except for a short expedition to Algeciras that June. This man wears a green coatee with red collar and cuffs, white lapels, yellow piping, gold epaulettes, and a black shako with silver lace. Watercolour by Antonio Pareira Pacheco. (Biblioteca Publica Municipal, Santa Cruz de Tenerife, Canary Islands)

Santa Fé Two-battalion regiment raised in the province of Granada from 1 September 1808. It was part of the Tarragona garrison, and was disbanded on 28 June 1811 on the city's surrender to the French. See illustration on page 44 for uniform.

Voluntarios de la Patria Three-battalion regiment raised in Nueva Castilla from 14 September 1808, it fought at Albuera and Saguntum in 1811, and was disbanded at the surrender of Valencia on 9 January 1812. Uniform as illustration on page 44.

Voluntarios Leales de Fernando VII Regiment of three battalions raised in Talavera de la Reina on 5 September 1808. It served in Extremadura, and one battalion was incorporated into other units in 1810. The other two fought at the siege of Alberquerque and were dissolved on the surrender of the city on 19 August 1811. Uniform as illustration on page 44.

La Muerte Single-battalion regiment raised in Galicia from 23 April 1809, and incorporated into the Lobera Regiment on 1 July 1810. Uniform as illustration on page 44.

Cazadores de Campo de Cariñena Light infantry battalion of 700 men raised in Aragon from 1 May 1809. It fought at Saguntum in 1811, and was incorporated into the Napoles Regiment on 2 March 1815. They were issued brown cloth for ponchos and white linen for shirts in September 1809.

Voluntarios de Molina Light infantry battalion of 800 men raised from 2 June 1810 in New Castille, it fought at Saguntum in 1811, and was incorporated into the Guadalajara Regiment on 2 March 1815. From 1809 to 1811 the uniform was a blue jacket with scarlet collar and linen pantaloons.

Cazadores de Soria This light infantry battalion of 600 men raised from 1 July 1810 in New Castille was incorporated into the San Marcial Regiment on 2 March 1815. They were issued brown cloth for ponchos and white linen for shirts in September 1809.

Legion Extremadura or **Legion Estramaña** This unit, proposed by John Downie, a romantic and wealthy British hispanophile, was approved by the Cortes in July 1810 and organized in southern Spain from September with 'a proportion of British officers to join and assist in the formation of the said Legion' (PRO, WO 1/1120). It was to have 2,400 light infantry in four battalions (six companies of 100 men each), 300 light cavalry in three squadrons, and 300 horse artillery. The British government supplied carbines and pistols, and swords for the mounted troops were delivered in England to Downie, while the infantry arms were issued from the stores in Portugal. It seems that the light artillery did not last very long. The cavalry was, in addition, armed with lances and thus became known as lancers.

LEFT **An officer of the Regimiento Ligero de Valencia, 1810. This regiment was part of the Cadiz garrison during 1810 and wore blue coatees with blue lapels, red collars, cuffs, turnbacks and piping edging the lapels, gold epaulettes, and black helmets with a white crest. Watercolour by Antonio Pareira Pacheco. (Biblioteca Publica Municipal, Santa Cruz de Tenerife, Canary Islands)**

RIGHT **Officer of the Regimiento de Guadix, 1810. This unit was organized in Granada from 10 August 1808, and consisted of one 1,200-strong battalion. It arrived in Cadiz on 27 May 1810, on its way to Huelva; and was eventually incorporated into the Rey Regiment in March 1815. The uniform is a blue coatee with red collar, cuffs and lapels, gold epaulettes, white breeches, and a black shako with silver lace and cords and a small silver plate. Watercolour by Antonio Pareira Pacheco. (Biblioteca Publica Municipal, Santa Cruz de Tenerife, Canary Islands)**

The unit saw much action and the Spanish were most grateful to the colourful Downie, even making him a gift of the Conquistador Pizarro's sword, which he carried into action – when he was captured by the French in 1812 he managed to throw it to safety. On 1 December 1814 the legion's mounted troops became a distinct regiment of cavalry, and on 1 June 1815 were renamed Lanceros de Extremadura. The light infantry battalions mustered about 2,000 men in 1811; by December 1814, when it became an independent infantry unit, the corps stood at 1,289 men, who sailed to Lima, Peru in January 1815.

Downie wanted his unit's uniform to reflect Spain's 'Golden Age' and proceeded to provide regimentals at his own expense: 'with a view to excite the National feelings of the Spaniards, I have had made upon the model of the ancient Spanish costume' – which, incidentally, cost Downie 'considerably more' than ordinary uniforms. It was white and scarlet with a short scarlet cape and a scarlet bonnet, but the actual appearance remains conjectural. This costume caused astonishment when Downie's squadrons arrived in Cadiz in 1811, and more conventional uniforms were thereafter procured. According to Clonard, from late 1811 to about 1814 the lancers wore a black shako with a yellow top band, a red pompon, a brass plate and chin scales; a blue coatee, with straw-coloured pointed cuffs, collar and turnbacks, green lapels, scarlet piping, brass shoulder scales and buttons; blue pantaloons with yellow stripe and brass buttons; blue housings edged with yellow lace and red outer piping. A red lance pennon was carried. The lancers were sent '600 pairs of Hessian boots' in December 1810 (PRO, WO 1/846).

The legion's modern infantry equipment consisted of British crossbelt accoutrements, knapsacks and shoes. The light cavalry had British saddles, holsters, carbine buckets, lance buckets, and shabraques with pouches, belts, boots and spurs for the troopers. The horse artillery had the same appointments as the cavalry with 'the addition of harness, &c., for the horses' (PRO, WO 1/1120).

Cazadores de Mallorca A light infantry regiment of 600 men raised on the island of Mallorca from 8 October 1811, commanded by Colonel Patrick Campbell. Its uniform was 'the same as the 95th Regiment', according to Woolcombe, and consisted of a green jacket with a black collar and pointed cuffs piped white, three rows of pewter buttons on the chest, green pantaloons, black short gaiters, a stovepipe shako with a tin buglehorn badge and a green plume, and black infantry accoutrements. The regiment was armed with muskets, not rifles. Officers would have had the green dolman with black collar, cuffs and cords and three rows of silver buttons on the chest, as worn by officers of the British 95th Rifles.

Cazadores de Cataluña This battalion of Catalonian chasseurs, also called Cazadores de Manso after their founder and commander José Manso, was raised from 30 June 1811 and had some 1,200 men in six companies, selected from the fittest so as to be very efficient and mobile. It became renowned for its hit-and-run tactics against French columns, who rarely caught up with Manso's men. At first the uniform was a brown greatcoat trimmed with green.

Artillery

In 1808 the Royal Corps of Artillery in Europe consisted of four regiments in Spain, apart from the batteries detached in Denmark, 15 garrison companies in various cities, brigades in Mallorca, Ceuta and the Canary Islands, the academy at Segovia and the corps general staff. Another large part of the corps was in America and the Philippines. The French invasion and occupation of the Iberian peninsula brought considerable disorganization to the corps which, although repeatedly transformed, continued to exist as a fighting force in spite of enormous difficulties over supplies, arms and training. While some companies of the corps and its general staff ceased to exist many new units came into being, such as the Brigade Maniobrera consisting of three horse batteries raised in Sevilla from October 1808. Indeed, many of the corps' disorganized companies reorganized themselves into mounted batteries serving with the regional forces. Others were part of volunteer units, such as the units raised in Cadiz, but were not part of the corps as such.

By 1810 most of the country was occupied by the French but, in late December, a fifth regiment was nevertheless organized on the island of Mallorca. In March 1811 the horse artillery was organized into four squadrons, while the five regiments were now solely composed of foot artillery. In April 1811 the corps was renamed *Cuerpo Nacional de Artilleria* by the Cortes in Cadiz, but the 'Royal' style continued to be used.

The uniform of the foot batteries consisted of a blue coat with blue lapels and cuff flaps, a scarlet collar with yellow grenade, scarlet cuffs and turnbacks and scarlet piping edging the lapels and cuff flaps; brass buttons; a blue waistcoat piped scarlet; blue breeches and knee-length black gaiters, later replaced by blue pantaloons and short gaiters. From 1808 to December 1811 the official headgear was the bicorn with yellow lace and a red plume, but illustrations, notably by Goddard and Booth, also show round hats with the brim turned up at the front or the side. Another English print by J.Booth shows the bicorn edged yellow, but the coatee lapels are red; this may have been a colourist's error, but there might be a basis to some detachments of Spanish artillery having red lapels. When on Mallorca in 1812 Lieutenant Woolcombe noted the uniform of the artillery as 'blue jackets and red facings (lapels), cuff and cape (collar)'. This would have been the 5th Regiment of the corps formed from December 1810.

The 1808 artillery regulations permitted the wear in warm climates of 'waistcoats, breeches or pantaloons of white linen...and a coat of the

Officer of the Royal Corps of Artillery, c.1809-1811, wearing a round hat with a red plume and the brim upturned at the side; a blue coat with blue lapels and collar, red piping, cuffs and turnbacks, gold buttons and epaulettes, a red waistcoat laced with gold, white breeches and black boots. (Print after Goddard and Booth)

same material with the cuffs and other distinctions as on the (blue woollen) uniform' of the corps. This was merely putting into regulations a practice which went back several decades.

In principle the horse batteries wore the same uniform as the foot companies, except that they had short-tailed coatees instead of coats. However, there were variations. The Maniobrera Brigade, for instance, had silver lace edging the lapels, white metal buttons and black leather caps with a black crest with brass fittings and a red plume. Others appear to have had fur busbies.

Officers had the same uniform, but of finer material with a gold collar grenade, epaulettes, lace and button. Their bicorn hats were laced with gold, and their shakos had gold lace and cords.

Volunteer artillery units did not belong to the Royal Corps and had their own uniforms.

Engineers and Sappers

In spite of considerable disruptions during the war of independence, the Royal Corps of Engineers and the Sappers and Miners were always found with the Spanish armies. Trained engineer officers were much in demand and schools were set up in Cadiz and Mallorca. Several other sapper units were spontaneously raised from 1808, some of which were grouped with the regular battalion in 1811 to form a new six-battalion *Regimiento de Ingenieros*, whose officers were no longer required to be from the Corps. The men were mostly sappers (sometimes called pioneers by the British), and while their officers might not be professional engineers, the regiment served under the general supervision of engineer officers.

Officers of the Royal Corps of Engineers wore the same uniform as previously (see MAA 321) in 1808. However, it was simplified from 1 March 1809 by replacing the white piping and violet facing with scarlet collars and piping, blue lapels, and the elimination of silver lace. In effect, the uniform was similar to that of artillery officers except for

RIGHT **A guerrilla seen near Ciudad Rodrigo by Bradford in 1809. He wears a wide-brimmed hat, a short jacket, breeches and an ample cloak, these homespun items usually being brown; and is shod with the characteristic *alpargatas* or tied-on sandals. He is armed with a musket and an antique-looking sword, and typically wears a 'belly box' for cartridges. (Anne S.K.Brown Military Collection, Brown University; photo R.Chartrand)**

LEFT **Guerrillas ambush a party of French light horse in a farm, c.1809-1812. (Print after L.Sergent)**

RIGHT **Francisco Espoz y Mina (1781-1836), 'Mina the Elder' – the most successful and important guerrilla leader of the war. This gifted tactician in hit-and-run warfare was also a good organizer and administrator; the best of his men eventually formed units of the regular army.**

silver buttons, hat lace and turret insignia at the collar. The Battalion of Sappers and Miners followed the same changes as the engineers in 1809, taking the scarlet collar and piping and blue lapels, and eliminating the white buttonhole lace. The Engineer Regiment formed in 1811 was to wear the same uniform as before, but instead of a turret badge on the collar a crossed pick and fascine badge was worn in silver or white.

GUERRILLAS

From the start of the French invasion small bands of patriots harassed isolated French parties using hit-and-run tactics. The concept caught on like wildfire and quickly became known as *'guerrilla'* – 'little war' – a term that has since become part of the universal language (although the form *guerrilleros* was sometimes used for those who waged it).

On 28 December 1808 the Central Junta recognized the value of these groups and issued instructions as to composition, pay, etc. The basic organization was to be 50 men 'more or less' in each *partida*, headed by a commandant, a second-in-command and three subalterns for foot troops and two for mounted units. Discipline was to be according to the royal regulations in force in the army. They had to find their own arms and clothing; were to harass enemy communications and messengers, and ambush small garrisons and isolated troops. Local juntas in Extremadura, Galicia and Asturias issued orders to the same effect, and this spread to the occupied provinces.

According to Lieutenant-Colonel Williams, '...in the whole of the northern and midland provinces, those patriot bands were denominated guerrillas; in the mountain districts included under the name of Serra de Ronda, in Andalucia, the irregular bands were termed *serranos*. The distinction was, that the guerrillas acted in concert, the *serranos* on his (sic) own responsibility. The dress of the guerrilla was a short jacket of russet brown, and leather leggings of the same dark colour; that of the *serranos* was velveteen, of an olive green colour, profusely ornamented with silver buttons, and his legs encased in leather boots. A belt of short leather surrounded the waist of each, stuck full of weapons of the French officers they had slain. When in small parties those predatory bands were called *partidas*.'

Many of their arms were captured from the French, some were home-made, and others came from Britain. Following the distribution of weapons to the bands of Mina, El Pastor and Longa, James Johnson, a British officer sent to meet them, reported in September 1811 that 'what these chiefs mostly complain of is the great want of clothing & shoes, their troops being in general, very ragged & barefooted.' Weapons were not

23

likely to be wanted in quantity 'for some time to come', but it was essential 'that they should be supplied, as early as possible with ammunition' (PRO, WO 1/261).

The French considered the guerrillas as bandits and rebels rather than soldiers, and capture often meant a French firing squad. Even family members of suspected guerrillas were imprisoned, deported or shot by the French in their efforts to intimidate patriots. This only increased Spanish determination and hatred, however, and some guerrillas consequently gave no quarter. Costello of the 95th Rifles recalled seeing '... a swarthy, savage-looking Spaniard... armed to the teeth with pistols, daggers and a long gun... together with his crimson sash and free bearing', taking out of a purse 'a number of human ears and fingers... cut off from the bodies of the French whom he himself had slain in battle, each ear and finger having on a golden ring. Napoleon, he observed... loves his soldiers, and so do the ravens.'

It is next to impossible to estimate the number of guerrillas under arms. It seems that some 58 groups were active in 1808, and 156 in 1810, decreasing to 35 by 1813. An estimated 25,000 guerrillas were active in northern Spain alone in 1810-1811, tying down up to 50,000 French troops by their activities. Some bands became veritable armies, with their own supply and pay systems. The principal ones are outlined below. They were always known by the names of their leaders, often unsavoury characters, but talented warriors and natural leaders of men. These men had considerable popular followings; many used *noms-de-guerre*, e.g. El Pastor ('the Shepherd'), El Medico ('the Doctor'), El Abuelo ('the Grandfather'), El Manco ('One-Arm'), Chaleco ('Waistcoat'), and even Calzones ('Breeches').

The value of guerrillas to Wellington's army was tremendous. The French officer J.J.Pellet possibly summed it up best by noting that 'the bands of Spanish insurgents and the English army supported each other. Without the English the Spanish would have been quickly dispersed or crushed. In the absence of the guerrillas, the French armies would have acquired a unity and strength that they were never able to achieve in this country, and the Anglo-Portuguese army, unwarned of our operations and projects, would have been unable to withstand concentrated operations.' To the Spanish, who saw their regular forces rep-eatedly defeated, the guerrillas' successes kept hope alive during their relentless fight for independence.

Juan Diaz Porlier, El Marquesito ('the Little Marquis') – so called

A rough impression of the dress purportedly worn for a time by some of the lancers of Don Julian Sanchez's band - captured (at least partial) uniforms of the Polish Lancers of the French Imperial Guard, in blue faced with crimson. Sanchez was one of the most feared guerrilla leaders; raised in Salamanca during 1808, his band waged a relentless struggle against the French, no quarter being asked or given. Besides practising guerrilla warfare, the unit participated in the defence of Ciudad Rodrigo in 1810, and fought at the battles of Salamanca (Los Arapiles), Vittoria and San Marial. (Print after E.Estevan)

1: Militiaman, Zaragoza, 1808-09
2: Fusilier, Extremadura Infantry Regt., 1808-09
3: Fusilier, Batallon Ligero de Zaragoza, 1808-09

A

1: Fusilier, 4th Marine Regt., c.1810-11
2: Fusilier, Almeria Regt., 1808-11
3: Fusilier, Castrapol Regt., 1809

1

2

3

B

WR/. 98

1: Fusilier, Mina's 1st Bn. of Alava, 1810
2: Guerrilla chief, c.1812
3: Trooper, Mina's Navarra Hussars, 1811-12

WRy. 98

C

1: Trooper, Coraceros Espanoles, 1810-11
2 & 3: Infantry fusiliers, northern Spain, 1810

D

1: Drum Major, Voluntarios de Madrid, 1811
2: Trooper, Daroca/Aragon Hussars, c.1811-13
3: Fusilier, 3rd Catalonian Legion, 1810

WRV. 98

E

1: Colonel, Cuerpo del Estado Mayor, 1810-15
2: Corporal, Alarmas Gallegas, c.1810-12
3: Gunner, Collure Artillery Cos., Alarmas Gallegas, c.1810-12

F

1: Infantry fusilier, eastern Spain, 1811
2 & 3: Infantry fusiliers, Andalucia, 1811

G

1: Fusilier, Toledo Regt., c.1811-13
2: Field officer, Numancia Dragoon Regt., c.1810-13
3: Gunner, Marine Artillery, 1810-15

H

This French print shows a motley array of military and regional costume worn by guerrillas. The arms were also quite varied, with belt pistols, various swords and a blunderbuss shown here. The figure in the centre may be a lancer of Don Juan Sanchez's band in c.1809 dress.

because he was the nephew of the famous Marques de la Romana – was a former officer of the regular army who took to the hills. His band of at least 1,000 men operated in La Mancha and the Asturias. In July 1809 Porlier planned to dress his cavalry in grey jackets and trousers with red cords and piping, and his infantry in brown coats with scarlet facings. In 1810 his band embarked on British ships, and captured several ports including Santona and Gijon. Between September 1810 and September 1811 Porlier's troops received '400 jackets, pantaloons, caps & cockades' with '500 muskets & bayonets' and 200 sabres from the British (PRO, WO 1/261).

Juan Martin Diez, El Empecinado ('the Obstinate'), had been a regular soldier and was a farm labourer when he decided to fight the French, following Fernando VII's detention by Napoleon in 1808. He intercepted French couriers in Guadalajara province, and within a few months was chief of some 1,500 guerrillas, eventually heading a respectable army estimated at 10,000 men by the French. His foot troops included the Siguenza Light Infantry Regiment, the Guadalajara Volunteers and the Molina de Aragon Volunteers. His cavalry, 'excellent and perfectly mounted' according to Hugo, consisted of the corps led by El Manco, Sardina, Mondideo and Don Damasco, his brother. He seized several French treasury convoys by daring ambushes in Old Castille, and three French battalions were captured when his guerrillas took Calatayud. In early 1811 the British managed to send 'for the use of the Spanish Patriots of Guadalajara, vizt., 2,000 muskets, pouches & sets of accoutrements; medicines and surgical instruments &c for 5,000 men, 2,000 blankets' (PRO, T 28/8). In December 1811 El Empecinado organized two regiments of mounted Cazadores of Madrid and of Guadalajara. From 1812 his troops became part of the regular army, and Diez was made a brigadier-general.

The guerrilla leader Don Juan de Palarea, 'El Medico', in the uniform of the Iberia Hussar Regiment c.1812. Raised in Vizcaya from 1 September 1811, the Iberia Hussar Regiment had 480 men in four squadrons. Their uniform was an all-crimson dolman, a blue pelisse edged with black fur, blue breeches, pewter buttons, white cords, a blue hussar sash with white barrels, and a black bearskin cap with a red feather and white cords; the saddle housings were blue edged with white lace. (Contemporary print)

Xavier Mina, El Estudiante ('the Student'), was only 18 when his father was arrested and the family estate in Navarra plundered during 1808. He procured a musket and a cartridge box, and with a few dozen men formed a guerrilla band in the mountains, 'distinguished by a red riband in their hats, and a red collar to their jackets' (Williams). His party soon grew to 1,200 men; but on 31 March 1809 Xavier Mina was captured by the French, and his band dissolved.

Francisco Espoz y Mina was Xavier Mina's uncle and had served in Doyle's Tiradores before joining his nephew's band. Following Xavier's capture Espoz y Mina rallied some of his men, and went on to become one of the most outstanding of the guerrilla leaders. Colonel Don Lorenzo Xeminez reported that:

'The French call Mina the King of Navarre... He never takes either a regular soldier, or a regular bred officer, into his corps... Whenever a volunteer of infantry joins Mina, he is not allowed to bring anything but a pair of sandals, half-stockings, breeches, and jacket... His arms are all rusty on the outside, but he is particularly careful to have them well cleaned within, and good locks and flints: his bayonets are encrusted with the blood of Frenchmen... he ordered all his men to put three musket-balls in each of their pieces... His cavalry, at this time, consisted of 150 intrepid and valiant men, dressed like hussars, with jacket and blue pantaloons; caps (shakos) like the rest of the army with this difference, that they have about a yard of red cloth hanging down their backs, in a point from the cap, and a gold tassel at the end. All of them wear sandals and spurs; and Mina himself never wears boots, or half-boots, but sandals, in order the more easily to escape, by climbing up the side of mountains, if he gets knocked off his horse...' (*Annual Register*, 1811).

By 1810 Mina had raised three infantry battalions of 1,000 men each, the battalions of Alava (see Plate C for uniforms). Some of the cloth, powder and weapons were bought in France and smuggled in by bribing French Customs officials, and other supplies were British. In July 1811 James Johnson distributed some to 'El Pastor, commanding the Volunteers of Guipozcoa (Guipuzcoa), to the number of 500, subject to the command of Mina... I gave them 100 muskets, 50 sabres, 10,000 ball cartridges, 5,000 pistol cartridges, 30 pistols, 1,000 flints, our pouches not being calculated for the sort of warfare carried on by the Guerrillas, he refused to take any' (PRO, WO 1/261). By his own account, Mina eventually raised, disciplined and maintained nine infantry and two cavalry regiments amounting to 13,500 men. From 1813 Mina exchanged the role of guerrilla leader for that of a leading general in the regular forces, and his troops became a regular division of the army. From 1809 to 1814 he lost some 5,000 men, but reckoned that he had cost the enemy about 26,000 killed and wounded and 14,000 prisoners.

Don Julian Sanchez, born in Salamanca, became a guerrilla leader in Old Castille. He 'first began his career as a pig-boy, but owing to some cruelties exercised on a branch of his family by the French, he took an inveterate hatred to them' and sought revenge. He waged a 'war to the death' with about 500 lancers on the plains of Leon, and was in regular communication with Wellington, to whom he sent captured despatches and valuable intelligence. His renown increased as did 'his sanguinary feats, and gradually collected a small band, then a body, and eventually commanded upwards of twenty thousand guerrillas, well armed, and

The guerrilla leader Don Juan Martin Diez, 'El Empecinado', c.1812. He apparently wears the uniform of the mounted Cazadores de Madrid, which he raised in late 1811: a green coatee with a scarlet collar, cuffs and piping, silver buttons and lace. (Museo de Ejercito, Madrid)

equipped with British arms and accoutrements, and who rendered more assistance to the cause of the British than all the Spanish troops besides', according to Edward Costello.

Sanchez's band was certainly much smaller than Costello's quoted figure, but probably numbered several thousands. During one especially daring ambush he captured the French governor of Ciudad Rodrigo. In November 1812 Rifleman Costello 'saw Don Julian Sanchez, the noted Guerrilla leader, linked in arm with the Duke (of Wellington)'. Don Julian was described as having a 'square well-set figure, dark scowl and flashing eyes of the Guerrilla.' Another British officer, Captain William Bragge, saw him near Salamanca in June 1812 and wrote that 'The Don himself wears a Pelisse like the 16th (British Light) Dragoons with an immense Hussar Cap and the Eagle of Napoleon reversed. In this dress, accompanied by two aides de camp equally genteel in Appearance, Twelve Lancers, a Trumpeter in scarlet on a grey Horse...' By then, his infantry were 'in English Clothing and the Cavalry, both Horse and Man, completely armed and equipped in the Spoils of the Enemy, so that it is next to impossible to distinguish Friend from Foe.'

When first organized from 1808 Sanchez's lancers had wide-brimmed black hats, grey jackets with red collars and cuffs, brass buttons, yellow lace at the chest buttonholes and edging the collar and cuffs, a red sash, grey or buff breeches, and blue housings edged yellow; they were armed with a lance, sabre and pistols. Later on they wore captured blue and crimson uniforms of Napoleon's Imperial Guard Polish Lancers. In 1811 some were seen by Kincaid wearing 'cocked hats with broad white lace round the edges, yellow coats with many more than buttonholes, red facings, breeches of various colours, and no stockings but a sort of shoe on the foot with a spur attached. Their arms were as various as their colours; some with lances, some with carbines...'.

Geronimo Merino, El Cura, was indeed a 'parish priest'. Revolted by the wanton brutality of the French, he raised a band which became the most famous in Old Castille. In July 1810 his men caused over 200 casualties to the 43rd and 44th Naval Battalions in an ambush near Soria; and in October they captured a vast convoy, depriving the French troops in Burgos of supplies for weeks.

REGIONAL VOLUNTEERS AND ARMED PEASANTRY

A multitude of city volunteer and armed peasantry units were raised during the Peninsular War. Some are listed below, but there were many more in all parts of Spain.

Aragon The Zaragoza units are illustrated in Plate A. Many other short-lived Zaragoza units were raised during the second siege, such as the Husares de Palafox formed in December 1808 and disbanded on 21 February 1809, the day of the city's surrender.

Elsewhere, the Volunteers of Teruel had two *tercios;* the 1st Tercio wore a blue jacket with scarlet collar, cuffs and front piping, buff breeches, and a black round hat with a brass plate bearing the city crest; the 2nd Tercio had violet instead of scarlet facings. They took the old

Spanish name of *tercio,* in reference to the famous infantry of the 16th century; each tercio was generally similar in size to a battalion.

Andalucia The important port city of Cadiz was besieged by the French from 1810 to 1812. The Urban Militia of 20 companies of 100 men each was mobilized to support the regular troops, and wore blue faced with red. They were joined by many volunteers – see accompanying illustrations.

The battalion of Voluntarios de la Real Maestranza de Ronda was raised at Malaga in June 1808, and wore a blue coatee with blue collar, scarlet cuffs and lapels, yellow buttonhole lace at cuffs and lapels, brass buttons, a white waistcoat and pantaloons, and a black round hat with red plume. In July 1808 the Voluntarios de Honor de la Real Junta de Malaga had a blue coat with red facings, buff breeches, half-boots, and a black round hat trimmed with gold.

In Sevilla, on 28 May 1808, five battalions of volunteers were raised and a sixth on 1 June. Only the uniform of the 6th Battalion is known: a brown coatee and breeches, green collar, cuffs and epaulettes, brass buttons, and a round hat with a short red plume. The Guardia Patria de Caballeria was a squadron of three companies of 183 volunteer cavalrymen organized in Sevilla from 28 May 1808. Their duties were to escort the Central Junta and its leaders, and to serve as messengers carrying the Junta's decrees. It was probably dissolved at the same time as the Junta in 1810. The uniform was the same as the royal guard, the *Guardia de Corps,* the bandoleer being scarlet with silver lace.

The Carmona Lancers, raised from 1 June 1808, became the 2nd Squadron of the Regiment of Volunteer Cavalry of Sevilla on 18 August. Incorporated into the Montesa Cavalry Regiment in 1811, the Carmona Lancers wore a brown jacket and gaiter trousers, green collar piped in white, arrowhead-style pointed cuffs and elbow patches, white buttonhole lace on the chest, pewter buttons, a white multi-pointed star on the collar, and a round hat with white headband and cockade loop.

Catalonia Tercios of volunteers styled *Miqueletes* were raised in Catalonia from 15 May 1808. At least 28 tercios were raised, most having about 800 men and being named after a locality. In many instances there were several tercios from a single town and its area, numbered e.g. 1st and 2nd Tarragona, 1st, 2nd and 3rd Vich, or 1st to 4th Lerida. All the tercios were incorporated into the 1st and 2nd Catalonian Legions on 7 November 1809, or else were lost at the fall of Gerona on 10 December 1810.

The dress of the units was recommended to be of the same colour, and styled in a fashion pleasing to the youths making up the units. Some units' uniforms are known. The 1st Tercio of Gerona had a brown jacket with cuff flaps and brown pantaloons, scarlet collar, cuffs and piping on the pantaloons, seven black hussar-style cords on the breast of the jacket, *alpargatas* sandals, and a round hat with a red plume. The 2nd Tercio had blue facings instead of scarlet, and the 3rd had green. The tercios of Vich had blue jackets and pantaloons, scarlet cuffs and piping, and a round hat with red and white plume.

A corps of Voluntarios de la Defensa de Barcelona was organized from 10 October 1808. It wore a scarlet coatee with yellow collar, cuffs and lapels, white lace edging the collar, cuffs and lapels, white buttonhole lace on the lapels, pewter buttons, tight white pantaloons piped

Officer of the Voluntarios Distinguidos de Cadiz, 1810. First raised with four companies from 2 June 1808, this unit expanded to four battalions of five companies each, mobilising nearly 2,000 men on 3 February 1809. It became a regiment on 3 February 1811, and served until the end of the war. The dress uniform was a scarlet coatee with green collar, cuffs and lapels, a narrow scarlet pointed collar patch, white piping, silver buttons, a white waistcoat and trousers, and a bicorn with a red pompon. Watercolour by Antonio Pareira Pacheco. (Biblioteca Publica Municipal, Santa Cruz de Tenerife, Canary Islands)

RIGHT **Officer of the Voluntarios Distinguidos de Cadiz, 1810,** in a different service uniform – brown, with buff lapels and collar and scarlet cuffs, the latter changing to buff in 1811. The jokers in Cadiz soon nicknamed their volunteers the *Guacamayos* after the colourful local macaws. Watercolour by Antonio Pareira Pacheco. (Biblioteca Publica Municipal, Santa Cruz de Tenerife, Canary Islands)

Officer of the Voluntarios Distinguidos de Cadiz, 1810, wearing the service dress: a brown coatee and trousers, scarlet collar and cuffs, silver cords, epaulettes, lace and buttons, a black shako with silver lace and plate with red-over-white plume. Watercolour by Antonio Pareira Pacheco. (Biblioteca Publica Municipal, Santa Cruz de Tenerife, Canary Islands)

scarlet, black short gaiters, and a round hat with a white band, a brass plate and a yellow plume tipped red.

From 7 November 1809 the troops serving permanently, especially the miqueletes, were reorganized in Lerida into an army of four Catalonian Legions. Each was led by a general officer and had two sections of infantry, a company of sappers, a company of infantry serving the artillery and two squadrons of light cavalry. A uniform is illustrated on Plate E.

On 29 May 1809 General O'Donnell ordered the formation of *Corregimiento* municipal units in Catalonia, generally consisting of two companies of light infantry tiradores per town. They were raised from volunteers who served for six months (sometime longer), and occasionally from regular line infantry units. On 13 November 1811 General Lacy ordered the reorganization of the corregimientos with the Reserve Army of Catalonia, each of the 14 units having five 100-men companies. Uniforms were not obligatory, but many wore a brown jacket without tails and with scarlet lapels, collar and cuffs, a scarlet waistcoat, brown breeches, brown leather gaiters, *alpartagas* sandals and a round hat. In November 1811 a new uniform was ordered, with each of the 14 town units assigned its own facing colour. This complicated system was apparently not adopted in practice, and the uniform worn was a brown jacket with scarlet collar and cuffs, with the town initials as a collar badge, and other items as before.

The Voluntarios Almogavares Battalion was raised in Ampurdan in the Gerona area during June 1810, the men in each company being armed with muskets except for six with a halberd and a blunderbuss, and two with an axe and a blunderbuss. Six men per company were mounted. The battalion was incorporated into the line infantry a year later. Uniforms were a blue jacket and breeches, scarlet piping, and a plain shako. Officers had a single-breasted coat with long tails, gold epaulettes and buttons.

Galicia The *Milicia Honrada de la Coruña* companies organized in 1808 wore scarlet coatees with green collars, cuffs and lapels piped white, brass buttons, the city's Tower of Hercules badge at the collar, and a round hat with a red plume. A Batallon Literario was formed from 22 June 1808 at Santiago de Compostela, the famous shrine of pilgrimage, from professors and students of the university; it had six companies of 130 *cadets escolasticos*, and was considered a light infantry unit. The uniform was a brown jacket and pantaloons, brown pointed cuffs piped yellow, yellow collar and aiguillette, brass buttons, and a round hat with a yellow band bearing the motto 'Viva Fernando VII'.

By the middle of 1809 the French had invaded much of Galicia and dispersed the regulars and volunteers. To counter the invaders, the *Alarma Gallega* (Galician Alarm) was established in almost every village and hamlet of the seven provinces of Galicia. At its peak in 1811 this force had up to 206,000 militiamen led by 6,000 officers (PRO, WO 1/261). Some would embody temporarily to watch French movements and take occasional shots at them. Artillery was sometimes used, and the Alarma had up to 138 light mountain pieces served by artillery detachments, some in uniform (see Plate F). The Alarma gradually dissolved from 1812 as the French retreated from north-western Spain.

Navarra At the beginning of the war in 1808 the Volunteers of Pamplona wore brown coatees and breeches, with a scarlet collar, cuffs, cuff flaps and lapels piped white, pewter buttons, and a round hat. With the French occupation Navarra became the domain of the powerful guerrilla bands under Espoz y Mina, so that many volunteers were part of his units.

Valencia Militia and Volunteers The *Milicias Honrada del Reino de Valencia* consisted of four battalions of militia formed in the city of Valencia by order of General José Caro at the end of 1808; a fifth Batallon de la Universitad was raised in 1810 at the university. Each battalion included a company of artillery. The uniform was a brown coatee with a red collar, cuffs and lapels piped white, red turnbacks, brass buttons, a white waistcoat, and black breeches. The 5th Battalion had a brass collar badge bearing the crest of the university.

From May 1808 and in 1809, several light infantry volunteer units were raised in Valencia such as the 1st, 2nd and 3rd Cazadores de Valencia, the 1st, 2nd and 3rd Cazadores de Orihuela, the Cazadores de Segorbe, and the Voluntarios de Alicante. From the latter part of 1810 to 1812 French forces occupied the area in strength and most units were wiped out. The 1st Cazadores de Valencia survived until March 1815, when it was incorporated into the Reina Regiment.

There appears to be little information on the specific dress of units. The light infantry wore a mixture of uniform and traditional rural folk dress consisting of a shako with a brass plate, red cords and bands, a blue jacket with a scarlet collar and pointed cuffs, blue wings criss-crossed with red tape, a red sash, white linen kilts (*zaragüelles*) instead of pantaloons, long stockings and *alpartagas* sandals (see illustration on page 46).

Offshore Islands and Presidios

Canary Islands The islands had their own regular battalion as well as units of provincial and local militias. The 800-man regular Canarias Battalion went to Cadiz in 1809, and became a regiment with a single battalion of six companies on 1 July 1810. It fought at Talavera in 1809, Albuera in 1811, Castalla in 1812, and grew to eight companies with the addition of a company of grenadiers and a cazador company on 8 May 1812. See the illustrations on pages 40 and 41 for uniform.

In 1808 the Provincial Militia organized an élite grenadier battalion. Its first uniform was a blue jacket and breeches, scarlet collar and cuffs, black gaiters, and a round hat with a red plume. Pacheco shows the grenadiers in 1810 wearing white and brown (see the illustrations on page 42). In 1809 the islanders sent the regular battalion and the grenadiers as reinforcements to Cadiz during March and April. Following the departure of these troops a Distinguished Militia Volunteer Battalion was raised in 1809; this wore a blue coatee and cuffs, with white lapels piped scarlet, scarlet collar and piping edging the cuffs, a round hat with a red plume at the left, and black accoutrements.

Mallorca This island was relatively untouched by the war until early 1811 when the British organized a large Spanish division under General Whittingham. It became a base to aid patriots on the mainland, the troops trained there eventually being landed in eastern Spain.

Ceuta & Mellila In 1808 the regular Fijo de Ceuta Regiment of three battalions was attached to the Army of Andalucia, but the 1st Battalion was sent back to Ceuta in December, two companies of grenadiers serving near Gibraltar from October 1809. On 1 July 1810 the regiment's Jbattalions were reorganized, each having four companies of fusiliers,

Officer of the Artilleros Distinguidos de Cadiz, 1810. Two companies were raised from 26 September 1808, and wore blue coatees and trousers with crimson collars, lapels and cuffs, white piping, silver epaulettes, gold buttons, and black shakos with gold lace and plates and red plumes. Watercolour by Antonio Pareira Pacheco. (Biblioteca Publica Municipal, Santa Cruz de Tenerife, Canary Islands)

RIGHT **Officer of the Bombarderos de Cadiz, 1810, also known as the Bombarderos de San Fernando. This one-company unit was raised in February 1810; the title of Bombardiers would indicate that it specialized in serving mortars. The service dress was a brown coatee and trousers with buff collar, cuffs and lapels, scarlet piping to facings and edges, gold epaulettes and buttons, and a black shako with gold lace and plate and a green-over-yellow pompon. Watercolour by Antonio Pareira Pacheco. (Biblioteca Publica Municipal, Santa Cruz de Tenerife, Canary Islands)**

This untitled figure may be a captain of the Cadiz Artillery serving Extramuros, or outside the walls, in 1810. He wears a white jacket and trousers, gold buttons and epaulettes, and a black round hat with a white or silver band. Watercolour by Antonio Pareira Pacheco. (Biblioteca Publica Municipal, Santa Cruz de Tenerife, Canary Islands)

one of grenadiers and one of cazadores. It was reduced to one battalion in 1812, which probably reflected the actual strength. The regimental dress apparently did not change, as the same uniform is recorded in the registers of 1808 and 1815: white coatee with white lapels, green collar, cuffs and piping, and pewter buttons.

Military Academies

Batallon de Voluntarios de Honor de la Universidad de Toledo/Colegio General Militar de Sevilla Raised in 1808 with students of the university of Toledo, it moved to Sevilla at the invitation of the Central Junta to escape the French occupation of Toledo in 1809, and was used as a guard to the Junta. Its graduates were commissioned in the Armies of Aragon and Navarra. It moved to Cadiz in 1810 and was incorporated into the San Carlos Military College.

Uniforms were coats of 'corinth' (a dark red with a brownish hue) with a scarlet collar, pointed cuffs and lapels, white turnbacks, white buttonholes on the lapels (two on each side of the collar – without buttons), white piping edging the lapels, cuffs and shoulder straps, silver buttons; white breeches, long black gaiters, and a black leather helmet with a black caterpillar crest, a narrow silver band, no plate, and a red plume.

Real Colegio de Preferentes de Granada Raised in 1808 from students of the university of Granada and housed in the convent of San Augustin; 36 officers graduated in late 1808. Incorporated into the Toledo school at Sevilla in early 1810. The uniform was a blue single-breasted coat and cuff flaps, green collar, red cuffs, white turnbacks, with white piping edging facings and front, silver buttons, aiguillette and epaulettes without fringes; white breeches, black long gaiters, and a bicorn.

Colegio Militar de San Carlos Also called **Colegio General Militar** and formed in Cadiz in 1810 from the Sevilla military schools, it consisted of 647 cadets, six companies of infantry, a company of cavalry and two guns for artillery drills. Uniforms were blue coatees with scarlet collars, cuffs and lapels, white buttonhole lace on lapels (two on each side of the collar and three on each cuff – without buttons), white turnbacks, waistcoat and pantaloons, silver buttons and aiguillette; and a shako with a silver plate, red pompon and white plume.

Academia Militar de Tarragona Formed in 1810, it consisted of 150 cadets, and helped in the defence of the city in 1811. It moved to Borjas and later to Poblet, and was reorganized as the Valencia Military School in 1814. The uniform was a blue coatee with blue collars, cuffs, lapels and turnbacks, white piping edging the facings, silver buttons and aiguillette; grey and white pantaloons, and a shako with a silver plate and a sky blue pompon.

Escuela Militar de Murcia Formed in 1810 with infantry cadets from the Army of Murcia, it had two companies of 80 and 100 cadets each. It was transferred to Cartagena in 1812, thence to Jaen, and incorporated into the San Carlos Academy in 1814. The uniform was a blue coat with blue cuff flaps, scarlet collar, cuffs, lapels and turnbacks, white buttonhole lace, white piping, silver buttons, epaulettes without fringes and aiguillette; a white waistcoat and pantaloons, and a shako with black cords and a white pompon.

Academia de Caballeria de San Felipe de Jativa Formed in 1810 with cavalry cadets from the Army of Murcia, it was incorporated into the

Military College of Murcia in 1812. The uniform was a blue single-breasted coat with scarlet collar, pointed cuffs and piping, sky blue three-pointed collar patches, silver buttons, epaulettes without fringes and aiguillette; blue pantaloons piped scarlet and strapped with leather, and a bicorn laced white.

Real Colegio Militar de Santiago Created in March 1811, consisting of 22 cadets who boarded at this college. The uniform was an all-blue single-breasted coatee, with red piping edging collar, cuffs, cuff flaps, down the front and turnbacks, gold buttons and aiguillette; white pantaloons, and a shako with a gilt plate and a red pompon.

Real Escuela Militar de Santiago Created in March 1811, this institution had three companies of cadets who lived out. The uniform was a blue coatee, with blue lapels and cuff flaps, a sky blue collar, cuffs, and piping edging the lapels and cuff flaps, silver buttons and aiguillette; white or blue pantaloons piped sky blue, and a shako with silver initials set within a scroll inscribed 'R.E.M.', a sky blue pompon, and black cords.

Real Colegio Militar de Olivenza Formed in 1810 with former cadets of the Literarios de Santiago and the Escolares de Leon battalions, it was incorporated into the Academy of San Fernando in 1812. The uniform was a blue coatee with red collar and cuffs, white lapels, white pantaloons, and a bicorn.

Real Colegio Militar de Palma de Mallorca Organized in 1812 as a one-company unit of 144 cadets, it was incorporated into the Tarragona Military College in 1814. The uniform was a blue coatee with yellow collar, cuffs and piping, silver buttons and aiguillette, a silver epaulette strap without a fringe on the right shoulder, white or blue pantaloons, and a bicorn.

THE NAVY

The French invasion of 1808 did not completely vanquish the remnants of the battered Spanish fleet. It managed to keep open some communications between Cadiz, the Navy's main base, and the Spanish colonies. The marine battalions saw a great deal of service alongside the army, fighting their country's former ally between 1808 and 1814.

Naval officers and sailors

The dress of naval officers did not change during this period, remaining as described in MAA 321. It is interesting to note the appearance of British-made Spanish Navy buttons from 1808. From the end of the 18th century Spanish sailors had a clothing issue, similar to the 'slop' clothing of other nations. It was, however, often of brown cloth as well as blue. In May and June of 1809 the provisional government in Cadiz issued instructions so that sailors on ships going to America would not be destitute. Every two years each sailor was to receive a cap, a jacket, a waistcoat, a pair of 'wide' trousers, shirts, stockings and shoes; the colour was to be that of the cloth furnished. An order of 24 June 1809 specified that the jacket and wide trousers were to be blue, the waistcoat white, and the cap blue; there was also a round hat of felt or straw.

While blue was worn by some crews, as was the case for the frigate

Officer, Batallon de Infanteria de Canarias, 1810. The battalion arrived in Cadiz from the Canary Islands on 24 April 1809, saw some inconclusive action during the Talavera campaign, and was ordered back to Cadiz in January 1810. The dress uniform shown was a white coat with red collar, cuffs, piping and buttonhole lace on lapels, green lapels and piping edging the collar and cuffs, silver epaulettes, white breeches, and a black shako with silver lace. Watercolour by Antonio Pareira Pacheco. (Biblioteca Publica Municipal, Santa Cruz de Tenerife, Canary Islands)

RIGHT **Campaign dress of an officer of the Batallon de Infanteria de Canarias, 1810. The brown jacket has red collar, cuffs, piping and buttonhole lace on the lapels, green lapels and piping edging the collar and cuffs, and silver epaulettes; it is worn with white breeches and a black shako with silver lace and a red plume. Watercolour by Antonio Pareira Pacheco. (Biblioteca Publica Municipal, Santa Cruz de Tenerife, Canary Islands)**

Perla, brown cloth was often used, no doubt because of supply problems. In 1810 the naval stores at Sevilla report over 2,000 brown sailors' jackets and trousers. In 1812 the standard sailor's dress was a brown jacket, brown trousers, serge waistcoat, striped linen shirt, blue cap and a pair of shoes. There was also a white linen jacket and trousers for hot climates (MN, Mss 1376 & 2311).

Marine Infantry and Artillery

From December 1806 there were only four marine battalions. However, in January 1809 the Navy regrouped and expanded its marine corps into five regiments of two battalions each; and a sixth regiment of three battalions was formed from that September. In July 1811 the 1st Battalion of the 4th Regiment was destroyed at Tortosa and its remaining companies were incorporated into the 5th at Cartagena.

The Marine Infantry's traditional uniform was blue faced with red, but because of shortages due to the French invasion uniforms tended to be plain during 1808-1812 (see Plate B). An order of 11 February 1813 decreed that the uniform of Marine Infantry regiments was to be a blue coatee with scarlet collar, cuffs, turnbacks and piping, blue three-button cuff flaps piped scarlet, three broad yellow laces on the chest, and brass buttons and anchors on the collar; blue pantaloons, and a stovepipe shako with a brass anchor and a short red plume. This elaborate uniform may only have been worn to a limited extent, however, since a clothing contract of November 1813 for the 1st Regiment specified an all-blue single-breasted coatee with brass anchors on each side of the collar, brass buttons, blue pantaloons, black half-gaiters and shoes. Headgear consisted of a shako and a blue forage cap piped scarlet with an anchor badge. The corps of Marine Artillery also simplified its dress (see Plate H).

Navy administration and medical staff

Naval administrative staff included intendants, commissaries, paymasters, accountants and storekeepers. These services were based in the Spanish ports that remained unoccupied by the French, such as Cadiz and colonial naval bases such as Havana, Cuba. In 1808 and for years to come these various officials had a basic common uniform: a blue coat and breeches, scarlet collars, cuffs, turnbacks and waistcoat, and gold buttons. Intendants had one row of broad gold twisted lace edging the coat, collar, cuffs and waistcoat, and a laced hat; commissaries and other officials had gold embroidered buttonholes on the coat and waistcoat, gold stars on the turnbacks, and an unlaced hat. From 10 July 1810 naval surgeons wore blue coats with scarlet collars, cuffs and lapels, gold buttons, no epaulettes, narrow gold lace edging the cuffs and collar, a white waistcoat and breeches, and a plain bicorn hat. There was also an elaborate system of lacing for professional staff at the Naval Royal Medical College in Cadiz.

Despite the angle this portrait is a useful source. It shows Colonel Mariano Gil de Bernabe, director of the Colegio Militar de San Carlos (also called Colegio General Militar) on the Isle of Leon, at Cadiz from April 1810 until his death in August 1812. He wears a blue coat with scarlet collar, cuffs and lapels, silver buttons and lace, and white waistcoat and breeches. (Museo de Artilleria, Segovia)

Officer in undress uniform, Batallon de Grenaderos de la Isla de Canaria, 1810. Brown jacket and trousers, red collar, cuffs and piping, and plain black round hat. Watercolour by Antonio Pareira Pacheco. (Biblioteca Publica Municipal, Santa Cruz de Tenerife, Canary Islands)

SELECT BIBLIOGRAPHY

Manuscripts
Many sources used for this study are from archival documents consulted at the Public Records Office (PRO), Kew, in the following classes of manuscripts: Audit Office (AO), Foreign Office (FO), Treasury (T), and War Office (WO); and at the Museo Naval, Madrid (MN), manuscript archives (Ms).

Books and articles
Barceló, Rubi, B., *El armamento portatil español (1764-1939), una labor artillera*, Madrid, 1976

Boletin de la Agrupacion de Muniaturistas Militares, Barcelona, Nos. 13-16, 1962

Brett-James, Antony, ed., *Edward Costello: Military Memoirs, Adventures of a Soldier*, London, 1967

Bueno, José M., *Uniformes Españoles de la Guerra de la Independencia*, Aldaba, 1989

Calama, Argimiro, *La Guerra de Independencia en Soria, La Rioja y Navarra*, Madrid, 1996

Calvo, Juan L., *Armamento reglamento y auxiliar del ejercito español*, Barcelona, 1975, Vol.1

Cassels, S.A.C., ed., *Peninsular Portrait 1811-1814: The Letters of Captain William Bragge, Third (King's Own) Dragoons*, London, 1963

Clonard, Conde de, *Historia Organica de la Infanteria y Caballeria Espanola*, 16 Vols., Madrid, 1847-1856, Vols.6 and 7

Dragona (became *Researching & Dragona* in 1995), all issues

Esdale, Charles J., *The Spanish Army in the Peninsular War*, Manchester, 1988

Gurwood, Lt. Col., ed., *The Dispatches of Field Marshal the Duke of Wellington*, London, 1838, Vols.V to VIII.

Hugo, A., *France Militaire*, 5 vols., Paris, 1833-1838, Vol.4

Mémoires militaires du Maréchal Jourdain, Paris, 1899

Oman, Charles, *A History of the Peninsular War*, London, 1903-1930 (r/p Greenhill), Vols.I to IV

Rodriguez Delgado, Ramon, *Historia de la Infanteria de Marina*, Andujar, 1927

Ruiz, Manuel Gomez, and Juanola, Vicente Alfonso, *El Estado Militar Grafico de 1791*, Madrid, 1997

Williams, Lt.Col., *The Life and Times of the Late Duke of Wellington*, London, 1853, Vol.1

Windrow, Martin, & Embleton, Gerry, *Military Dress of the Peninsular War*, London, 1974 (p/bk r/p 1997)

Officer, Batallon de Grenaderos de la Isla de Canaria, 1810. The Canarias Provincial Militia formed a battalion of grenadiers in 1808 which arrived in Cadiz on 29 March 1809. Deployed to help serve the city's artillery, it won distinction for its services in the forward batteries and at the battle of Chiclana in 1811. The uniform consisted of a white jacket and trousers, red collar, cuffs and piping, gold epaulettes, and a plain black round hat. Watercolour by Antonio Pareira Pacheco. (Biblioteca Publica Municipal, Santa Cruz de Tenerife, Canary Islands)

THE PLATES

A1: Militiaman, Zaragoza, 1808-1809

On 21 February 1809 the half-destroyed city of Zaragoza at last surrendered. Henri de Brandt, a Polish officer with the French army, recalled the scene: 'We had been there for an hour when the first elements of those who had so valiantly defended Zaragoza appeared. They were mostly youths of sixteen to eighteen years old, without uniforms, wearing grey greatcoats and red cockades. While casually smoking their cigarettes, they lined up in front of our ranks. The majority of the troops followed them closely. These were men of all ages and all conditions. A few had uniforms but the greater number wore peasants' clothes... The officers were only distinguished from their men by being mounted on mules and wearing large bicorns and long cloaks'. This must be one of the earliest mentions of cigarettes.

A2: Fusilier, Extremadura Infantry Regiment, 1808-1809

Over 600 men of the regiment were part of the Zaragoza garrison and were practically wiped out during the second siege. At this time most of the older regiments in the army still wore the 1805 regulation uniform (see MAA 321), which for Extremadura was white with crimson collar, cuffs, cuff flaps, lapels and piping with brass buttons, a bicorn with red plume and black gaiters.

A3: Fusilier, Batallon Ligero de Zaragoza, 1808-1809

Three battalions numbered 1st to 3rd, each of 600 men and 20 officers, were raised in Zaragoza from 1 June 1808. They fought heroically during both sieges of the city, being destroyed in the terrible second siege ending in February 1809. The uniform was a blue coatee with a scarlet collar with two white laces (no buttons), scarlet turnbacks, sky blue lapels and cuffs piped white, blue breeches, and a round hat with a white band. (J.M.Bueno, *Uniformes...*)

B1: Fusilier, 4th Marine Regiment, c.1810-1811

In May 1810 the men of the 2nd Battalion of the 4th Marine Regiment at Cartagena were issued a blue jacket with no lapels or turnbacks, green collars and cuffs, a white waistcoat and breeches, stockings of various colours and half-gaiters. They probably also had round hats, brass buttons and a brass anchor collar badge. (MN, Ms 1376)

B2: Fusilier, Almeria Regiment, 1808-1811

This two-battalion regiment was organized in September 1808 from the 3rd Battalion of the Zaragoza Regiment and the Volunteers of Granada. It took part in the defence of Barcelona in December 1808 and later saw much action in Aragon and Catalonia. It was destroyed in desperate defensive fighting during the French assault on Tarragona on 28 June 1811. The uniform was a brown coatee with scarlet collar, cuffs, lapels and piping, brown pantaloons, a round hat (perhaps with the brim turned up on the left) and a yellow cockade loop, and black accoutrements. (Conde de Clonard, *Historia Organica...*, Vol.8)

B3: Fusilier, Castrapol Regiment, 1809

This single-battalion regiment of 840 men was raised from 27 May 1808 in Asturias, and expanded to two battalions from October. It fought at Espinosa on 11 November, Neibla and Albuera in 1811, at the sieges of Tarragona, Tortosa and Pamplona in 1813, and crossed into France in 1814. It was incorporated into the Walloon Guards on 24 August 1815.

Sergeant Juan de Murias recalled that in May 1809, while with the Asturias army at Contrueces, Gijon, the regiment was issued British-made white jackets with scarlet collars, cuffs and piping, gold buttons, white breeches, and white forage caps with a red band. (Juan de Murias, *Historial del Regimiento de Castropol*, 1815)

C1: Fusilier, Mina's 1st Battalion of Alava, 1810

Don Francisco Espoz y Mina's three guerrilla battalions wore a black round hat with a scarlet cockade, a brown jacket with

At left, a trooper of the Coraceros Españoles, 1810; see Plate G for uniform colours. At right, a lancer of Downie's Extremadura Legion, 1811; he wears a blue coatee with yellow pointed cuffs, collar and turnbacks, green lapels, scarlet piping, brass shoulder scales and buttons; blue pantaloons with a yellow stripe and brass buttons; and a black shako with a yellow top band, a red pompon, brass plate and chin scales. The housings are blue edged with yellow lace and red outer piping; the lance pennon is red. (Print after Gimenez & Clonard)

collar, cuffs and lapels of crimson for the 1st, green for the 2nd, and yellow for the 3rd, pewter buttons, short brown pantaloons, woollen stockings and *alpartagas* sandals. The men were mostly armed with French muskets, and had black or brown ventral cartridge boxes. Linen hunting haversacks were carried at the side. (A.J.Carrasco Alvarez, 'La Militarizacion de las Guerrillas', *Dragona*, March 1995)

C2: Guerrilla chief, c.1812
Guerrillas might be ragged, but often dressed in dashing styles if they could. Based on a Dennis Dighton watercolour caricature in the Royal Collection of 'José de Espin, one of Don Juan Martin's chiefs', the figure has a green jacket with black collar and cuffs, silver piping, lace, and death's-head collar badges, silver buttons, black trousers with small silver buttons, and a greyish round hat with a silver plate and badge.

C3: Trooper, Navarra Hussars, 1811-1812
The Husares de Navarra were raised from 1 January 1811 by Espoz y Mina, with an establishment of four squadrons totalling 480 men. It was incorporated into the Calatrava Cavalry Regiment on 27 September 1815. This figure is based on a Dennis Dighton watercolour in the Royal Collection showing a 'Dragoon' (who is of course a hussar) of 'Don Mina's Corps'. The uniform was an emerald green

New Spanish infantry regiments raised in 1808 and 1809; from left to right:
Voluntarios de la Patria - green coatee with green lapels, cuffs and turnbacks, scarlet collar and cuff flaps, yellow piping, brass buttons, white waistcoat and breeches, and shako with brass plate, yellow band and cords and red plume.
Leales de Fernando VII - sky blue coatee and trousers with scarlet collar, cuffs and piping, pewter buttons, and shako with brass plate, yellow band and cords and red plume.
Officer, Santa Fé - sky blue coat, waistcoat and trousers, green cuffs and lapels, violet collar, cuff flaps and piping, silver buttons and epaulettes, and shako with silver plate and band and red pompon.
La Muerte - green coatee with blue collar, cuffs and piping, pewter buttons, grey trousers, and shako with white metal death's-head, red cockade and green pompon.
Voluntarios de la Victoria - brown coatee and breeches, scarlet collar bearing brass anchor badge, scarlet cuffs and lapels, brass buttons, tan gaiters, and black round hat with brass plate and red cockade.
La Patria, Fernando VII and La Muerte appear to wear French-style tan hide knapsacks with blue/white ticking rolls, and La Victoria a brown blanket strapped into a horseshoe shape; the muskets appear to be French. (Print after Gimenez & Clonard)

dolman with scarlet collar and cuffs, white cords, pewter buttons, blue overalls with a red stripe and black leather strapping, and a shako with white bands.

D1: Trooper, Coraceros Espanoles, 1810-1811

The 'Spanish Cuirassiers' were organized on 24 May 1810 in Reus, Tarragona, with an establishment of six companies of 70 men each, divided into two squadrons. The unit fought with distinction in several engagements. They were equipped with weapons, cuirasses and helmets captured by the Numancia Dragoon Regiment from the French 13th Cuirassiers at the battle of Mollet in 1810, though only one squadron received the cuirass and helmet. The uniform was a red coatee with green collar and cuffs, white piping and turnbacks, pewter buttons, white pantaloons, black high boots and a white cape. The white sheepskins were edged with red 'wolfsteeth', and the green housings with white lace. The Coraceros Españoles Regiment was amalgamated into the Reina Cavalry Regiment in 1818. (Conde de Clonard, *Album de la Caballeria...*)

D2 & D3: Infantry fusiliers, northern Spain, 1810

These figures are based on a British shipment sent to Coruña 'for the use of the Spanish armies in Galicia Leon and Castille', including 14,000 grey jackets, 6,000 blue jackets, 20,000 grey pantaloons and 20,000 shakos and cockades. The shakos sent from England had cockades but no plates. Muskets with bayonets and black accoutrements were also sent. (PRO, AO 16/61)

E1: Drum Major, Voluntarios de Madrid, 1811

Two regiments numbered 1st and 2nd were raised from 15 July 1808, but the 1st was incorporated into the Tiradores de Cadiz Regiment on 1 March 1809. The other served on as a

A range of guerrilla costumes, according to a French print. The better-dressed figure at the left is clearly a leader, shown with a couple of his men; the central figure may have some remnant of military uniform or at least urban dress, while the other wears the most basic peasant costume.

light infantry unit and was retained in the regular peacetime establishment in 1815. In February 1811, the regimental drum-major was assigned a blue coat with scarlet collar, cuffs, lapels and turnbacks, gold buttons and gold lace trim (MN, Ms 1376).

E2: Trooper, Daroca/Aragon Hussars, c.1811-1813
A group of horsemen, mostly from the Rey Dragoon Regiment who had escaped from Zaragoza, served attached to the Cariñena Infantry Regiment from April 1809. They were reorganized as the squadron of Daroca Hussars on 30 April 1810 by the order of the Junta of Aragon, augmented to two squadrons in August. The unit was renamed Husares Provinciales de Aragon, with four squadrons, on 6 April 1811. They saw much action in Aragon and, from 1811, in Valencia. The unit was attached to Whittingham's Division on 2 March 1813, and incorporated into the Almanza Hussars and Cazadores de Olivenza on 30 April 1813. From 1811 to 1813 they wore blue dolmans with scarlet collar and cuffs, white cords and lace, pewter buttons, pantaloons probably blue, a Tarleton-style helmet of black leather with a black crest, and a brown cape with red collar and linen lining. (Luis Serando Muzas, 'El Escuadron de Husares...', *Dragona*, Jan. 1994)

E3: Fusilier, 3rd Catalonian Legion, 1810
The four Catalonian Legions raised from the end of 1809 had sky blue coats and pantaloons, white waistcoats, pewter buttons, no gaiters, and round hats. The coat had distinctive facings as follows: 1st Legion, scarlet lapels, collar, cuffs and piping; 2nd Legion, sky blue lapels, scarlet collar, cuffs and piping; 3rd Legion, black lapels, collar and cuffs, scarlet piping; 4th Legion, sky blue lapels, black collar and cuffs, scarlet piping. Light infantry units in the legions wore the same, but had short-tailed coatees instead of long-tailed coats. The sappers had yellow lapels, collars and cuffs. The light cavalry had sky blue dolmans, pantaloons and capes, with black collar and cuffs for the 1st Squadron and crimson for the 2nd. (José Almiral & Ramon Soler, 'Legion Catalanas...', *Boletin de la Agrupacion...*, No. 3, 1962)

F1: Colonel, Cuerpo del Estado Mayor, 1810-1815
For full dress General Staff Corps officers wore a blue single-breasted coat with sky blue collar and cuffs edged with gold lace, gold buttons, a sky blue sash around the waist, a white waistcoat and breeches, and blue pantaloons when mounted. On campaign, these officers could also wear a blue dolman with sky blue collar and cuffs edged gold, three

OPPOSITE **Navy Brigadier Juan Gutiérrez de la Concha, c.1809, wearing a blue coat with scarlet collar, cuffs, lapels and turnbacks, gold lace edging the collar, cuffs and lapels, and gilt buttons. The rank is shown on the cuffs: three gold laces for a captain below a silver embroidered lace for a brigadier. (Museo Naval, Madrid)**

RIGHT **Spanish Navy buttons. Top row, left to right: gilt Spanish made, gilt British made, gilt British made. Bottom row, left to right: brass Spanish made, gilt British made, gilt British made. (Collection & photo John Powell)**

LEFT **Left, a light infantry Volunteer of Valencia, c.1810-1814, wearing the regulation shako and jacket mixed with regional costume, as described in the text. At right is an officer of the Royal Corps of Artillery. (Print after Martinet)**

rows of gold buttons in front, and black hussar-style cords. Their headgear would have been a bicorn hat laced with gold for dress, and a plain bicorn in the field.

F2: Militia Corporal, Alarmas Gallegas, c.1810-1812
In February 1810 the Galician Alarm issued a set of instructions. While almost everyone was dressed in civilian and peasant costumes, it recommended that all should wear the Cross of Santiago on the breast of their coats, in gold lace for a commandant, silver lace for his subaltern officers, red cloth for a captain (sergeant), and white for a corporal. The rest of the men were to have the red cross on the upper left sleeve. In 1811 the armed Interior Divisions of the Alarmas had 13,920 muskets, 12,940 carbines and 31,130 knives (PRO, WO 1/261).

F3: Gunner, Collure Artillery Companies, Alarmas Gallegas, c.1810-1812
The three artillery companies at Collure (Betanzos) even had a uniform, approved by the Junta, consisting of a brown round jacket and breeches, with yellow collar and cuffs, gold grenades at the collar, brass buttons, black knee gaiters, and a black round hat. Note the belly pouch with brass pricker, and a pistol hooked to the belt on the right hip; and see above for sleeve badge.

G1: Infantry fusilier, eastern Spain, 1811
In late May 1811 '8,000 suits of light blue clothing and 12,000 pairs of half-gaiters, ordered last December for the corps to be raised in Majorca' were shipped from Britain. Of these, there were 5,112 jackets, waistcoats and pantaloons intended for infantry of the line, including 2,587 suits having red facings and '2,525 suits faced with yellow'. This clothing

appears to have been sent on to the east coast of Spain along with arms for units forming there. No shakos were mentioned, so round hats were probably used. (PRO, FO 72/108 and WO 1/885)

G2 & G3: Infantry fusiliers, Andalucia, 1811
From June 1811 some '3,000 suit of blue clothing', to have 'one half faced with red and the remainder with yellow', went to Cadiz for issue to an unnamed 'particular corps of Spanish Patriots'. An ample supply of calico shirts, half-stockings and shoes was also supplied, but no shakos; thus round hats were probably worn. (PRO, WO 1/849 and 885)

H1: Fusilier, Toledo Regiment, c.1811-1813
Having fought at Talavera in 1809, at the Lines of Torres Vedras in 1810, and Albuera in 1811, their uniform had changed from white to a brown coatee with yellow collar, cuffs, lapels and turnbacks, pewter buttons in pairs, tight white pantaloons and black half-gaiters. This uniform changed again to blue in about 1813-1814. (Watercolour by Dennis Dighton, Royal Collection)

H2: Field officer, Numancia Dragoon Regiment, c.1810-1813
If many Spanish soldiers went in rags for lack of uniforms, this figure of an officer, based on an early French print, shows that some could be quite dashing when they found the resources. The old yellow coat and bicorn have been exchanged for a green uniform faced with white, laced with gold, and a crested helmet. A crimson or red sash – not used by Spanish officers for a century – is worn possibly in imitation of British and Portuguese officers. The regiment was nearly wiped out in the two sieges of Zaragoza, but was reorganized in Valencia in the spring of 1809, moved up to Catalonia in July, and fought many skirmishes there. It also fought at the battle of Sagunto in October 1811, and served in the Alicante, Murcia and Lerida areas from 1812 to the end of the war. (E.Gavira y Perez de Vargas & S.Marcos Rodriguez, *El Regimiento 'Numancia' en la Historia de España*, 1992)

H3: Gunner, Marine Artillery, 1810-1815
From November 1810 to 1815 the Marine Artillery wore a blue single-breasted coatee with scarlet collar and cuffs, brass buttons, a white waistcoat, blue pantaloons, black gaiters and a round hat. The coatee collar was ornamented on each side with a yellow flaming grenade. The corporals had gold lace edging the cuffs, the *condestables* or sergeants had gold-fringed epaulettes, and the drummers had livery lace on the cuffs only (MN, Ms 1376).

INDEX
Figures in **bold** refer to illustrations.